THE LITTLE BOOK OF

Angel Healing

THE LITTLE BOOK OF

Angel Healing

FIRST AID FROM THE HEAVENLY REALMS

Kimberly Marooney, PhD   *Foreword by Jean Slatter*

HAMPTON ROADS

Cover design by Kathryn Sky-Peck
Cover photograph "Cupid and Psyche," c.1865 (w/c, bodycolour and pastel
    on paper mounted on linen), Burne-Jones, Edward Coley (1833-98) /
    Yale Center for British Art, Yale Art Gallery Collection / Mary Gertrude
    Abbey Fund / Bridgeman Images
Interior by Deborah Dutton
Typeset in Adobe Garamond Pro, Bickham Script and Futura Std

Hampton Roads Publishing Company, Inc.
Charlottesville, VA 22906
Distributed by Red Wheel/Weiser, LLC
www.redwheelweiser.com

Sign up for our newsletter and special offers by going to
www.redwheelweiser.com/newsletter.

ISBN: 978-1-64297-002-9
Library of Congress Cataloging-in-Publication Data available upon request.

Printed in the United States of America
MAR
10 9 8 7 6 5 4 3 2 1

As I experience grace,
I strive daily to live upward each moment
into this infinite supply of love, wisdom, healing,
and everything that is streaming in from
the angels and the heavenly realms.

I dedicate The Little Book of Angel Healing
to all light workers, angel lovers, and healers
who are with me on this journey
into wholeness.

You are the blessing.

—Kimberly

Contents

Foreword
Angels to the Rescue

Do you believe angels can intervene on our behalf? I have heard countless stories of divine assistance that have affected me at a deep level. One such story brings tears to my eyes every time I think of it.

A mother recounted how she and her two-year-old son were admiring a parked fire truck. They crossed the street to go about their business, and then the unthinkable happened. The mother turned and saw her son running back across the street toward the fire truck and a car barreling down upon him. The impending accident was certain. It was an endless moment of anguish, panic, and pain that no mother ever wants to experience.

"Please God, NO!" was her only thought. Simultaneously with that thought, she saw an angel swoop down and catapult her son back into her arms with such force that they both fell backward. They held onto each other, crying with utter emotional relief as the full impact of what had happened came to their awareness.

Later that night when she was tucking her son in bed, her son said, *"Mommy, did you see me fly?"*

Spectacular stories such as this one warm our hearts and inspire our faith in miracles. However, we have come to believe that the powers of the universe are reserved for breathtaking rescues and other deeds of heroic proportion. What about smaller, less dramatic needs? Can angels be called upon to support us in healing common problems of ordinary life?

Many religions tell us that God is within. Daytime talk shows remind us to connect with Spirit. Dozens of best-selling authors encourage us to access our divine guidance. But how many of us know how to call forth the healing power of angels?

Kimberly Marooney's book will show you how to ask for and receive angel assistance for the struggles of everyday life. Believe it or not, our angels and all of the spiritual realm *want* to be included in every aspect of our lives. They *want* us to call upon them. They are eager for us to know that their loving energy is available to us anytime, anywhere, in any situation.

Do you need help with a health issue? Do you feel overwhelmed and stressed? Is your life falling apart? Are you sinking into sadness and depression? Is food addiction ruining your life? Are you longing for a soul mate? Do you want a closer relationship with the Divine? Is grief or resentment eating you up? Do you feel stuck? Blocked? Alone?

Angels to the rescue! Simply locate in this book the angel remedy for your concern and discover what everyday miracles are all about.

Heavenly help is an unconditional gift offered to us by a benevolent universe. Open your eyes and you will see evidence of the miraculous. You *do* have access to angel healing—a gift given to you by the heavens, and one you are expected to use with great joy for the highest good of all.

Now that's magic!

—Jean Slatter, best-selling author of *Hiring the Heavens: A Practical Guide to Developing Working Relationships with the Spirits of Creation*

A Divine Invitation

We are invited into the embrace of angels.
Who could resist such a divine invitation?
That narrows down our choices.
We can answer the calling joyfully,
celebrating every step of the journey,
or be carried on a stretcher
to the heavenly realms of healing.

A DIVINE INVITATION

One morning not so long ago, Archangel Raphael entered my meditation in answer to my prayer. "Just tell me what to do!" I implored him. I was struggling with a persistent health challenge and was tired of it. His presence wasn't surprising. I'm blessed with the continual presence and guidance of angels. The surprise was the message Raphael gave me and where the energy contained in the words took me.

With his message, I could see, hear, feel, and receive the benediction the words described in a more profound way than usual. I was in a divine Healing Clinic, surrounded by light beings infusing my light body into my physical body and life. In a few moments, I was profoundly healed and elevated in consciousness. That experience was my call to action to cocreate *Angel Healing* with Archangel Raphael, the Master Healer. The clinic where I was healed is the same that is offered to you in these pages. It is always open for you.

Millions of people throughout our beloved world are asking, crying, and praying, *"Just tell me what to do!"*

Are you one of us? The challenges of life can be overwhelming. We weren't meant to make life work without celestial support. Overwhelm and stress result when we think we have to figure everything out ourselves.

HEAVENLY FIRST RESPONDERS

Each one of us has access to divine healing, and angels are our first responders. No matter what you are facing in life, you can be restored and rejuvenated through personal experiences with angels.

Angels support the changes taking place on every level of life. Angelic intervention activates higher learning and consciousness needed to revitalize life on our planet in these remarkably challenging times.

You have received "A Divine Invitation." You may joyfully embrace angelic experiences in some areas of life and be carried on a stretcher to the heavenly realms of healing in other areas. This proves how well loved you are!

How do angels affect such astonishing results?
A guided journey into Archangel Raphael's Healing Clinic, the primary remedy, draws you into the heavenly realm where you meet your angel team. You will learn to activate your divinity, discover how you are the blessing, and align with your Master Self to access healing energy. Here, we explore the question, *"What more is possible for me now?"*

By identifying life problems that need attention, or "symptoms," then taking systematic action in the form of specific spiritual practices revealed in the Thirty Personal Angel Healing Remedies, you can reconstitute health, balance, love, and abundance through your divinity.

Angel Healing is not about relieving symptoms, finding a work-around, or even creative thinking. As you will experience in your journey to the Healing Clinic, an angel healing is a personal experience of divinity. Through experiencing heavenly energy, your symptom is brought into alignment with your soul calling, as directed by your Master Self.

> Optimal health, abundance, fulfillment, divinely loving relationships, and eternal peace are the result.

Angel Healing returns you to a sacred state of oneness with your Master Self.

ANGEL HEALING REMEDIES

A Hebrew tradition tells that soon after Adam was driven from the Garden of Eden, he experienced illness. The angel Raziel gave Adam a book listing all the medicinal herbs that could cure every possible illness. See how much we are loved? Even before illness manifested, the cure was created.

—Kimberly Marooney from *Angel Blessings: Cards of Sacred Guidance and Inspiration*

If you knew how much the angels have to give you, you would be amazed! Everything we need is available even before we recognize the need. Let's explore the Angel Healing Remedies so you know how to access this treasury of muchness.

Each Angel Healing Remedy tells a story that you may relate to. Angels enter the story bringing wisdom, guidance, and resources. The Angel Prescription describes actions you can take to expand your perspective of this symptom or topic. When you enter into higher consciousness, new possibilities come into view. You have the ability to see your symptoms as an opportunity to leave behind old beliefs and habits. You are awakening the essence of your Master Self.

To use your personal Angel Healing Remedies,

1. Identify your *symptom* or situation in life that needs attention.
2. Find the *Angel Healing Remedy* that most closely matches your need.
3. Take the *Angel Prescription.* Read the full remedy and do the exercise!
4. Linger in the *Angel Blessing* energy to complete the healing.

It's that simple.

Think of this book as your personal healing session with the angels. Read straight through to experience the progression of healing, or pick the remedy you most need.

SYMPTOMS

Symptoms are real-life challenges that guide us to qualities we want to enhance in ourselves, as well as situations we need to counter or release.

In medicine, symptoms are defined as subjective evidence of disease or disturbance, such as a headache or a fever. Rather than focus on a diagnosis of disease, *Angel Healing* focuses on what is lacking ease and situations that are troublesome. Symptoms may also be invitations to greater good.

A symptom, for our purposes, points to the existence of something else:

- Health issues may be a symptom that an old belief needs to be released to embrace a deeper truth.
- An unwelcomed shift at home or work hints that a new opportunity, more closely aligned with your heart and soul, is possible.
- Financial distress may be forcing you to transform false beliefs of scarcity into abundance.
- Your heart may be aching for your soul mate, a symptom that the deeper longing is for divine love.
- Or, your soul is calling you to share your gifts and wisdom in a much bigger way.

The circumstance of your life, coupled with the deep yearning of your soul, reveals where you are embracing Spirit or being carried on a stretcher to the heavenly realms of healing.

Angels are the fast track. When angels touch your life, you are restored to wholeness. Once you have made the connection, angels go before you *preparing the way for a loving, vibrant, abundant, creative, and fulfilling life of joy.*

How do you make this connection? Healing means becoming whole. Think of an Angel Prescription as first aid that uses angel interactions, wisdom, and spiritual practices to restore your wholeness.

ANGEL PRESCRIPTIONS

A *prescription* is defined as an instruction written by a practitioner, authorizing the patient to receive medicine or treatment. Angel Prescriptions focus on taking spiritual treatments to restore wholeness.

As humans, we have been trained to look for symptoms. We are well aware of the forces that are at play in our lives. Then what? We often get stuck here, or we lack a systemized framework to respond to, or treat, these recurring issues.

Over my thirty plus years as a minister, spiritual counselor, and angelologist, I've heard stories from thousands of people around the world. From these stories, I've compiled our most common situations. I say "our" because I've personally been in each of the situations that follow. They have been carefully selected as our collective highest priorities in life. They are the same challenges and opportunities that have shaped my spiritual experiences and me! My darkest and most persistent challenges have become my greatest blessings, demanding that I strengthen the qualities of my soul needed to respond, effectively improving my life.

Stroll through your personal Angel Healing Remedies, looking for the story that most closely matches your need. As angel mystic Kimberly, I've shared wisdom from the angels. As Dr. Kimberly, I'm the practitioner writing the angel prescription. And as Rev. Kimberly, I've added a blessing to each of the stories.

ANGEL BLESSINGS

The Angel Blessing guides you into a personal experience of how much the angels care for you. By reading the Angel Blessing with an open heart, you will "know" that angels are always present, providing opportunities for divine intervention.

Each Angel Remedy is your call to action, guiding you into direct, personal experiences with angels and your Master Self that restore peace, rejuvenate your body to health, correct conflict and misunderstanding in relationships, provide creative substance, relieve challenging situations, and offer solutions that never would have occurred to you. These results are *Angel Healing.*

Read on for your first personal experience of Archangel Raphael's Healing Clinic.

Your Personal Angel Healing Remedies

1.

ARCHANGEL RAPHAEL'S HEALING CLINIC

Just tell me what to do!

How many times have you felt like that? You have a problem and just want to know what to do to make it better or go away.

Take this journey with your angels into Archangel Raphael's Healing Clinic.

During this journey, you will meet your angels, learn to activate your divinity, discover how you are the blessing, and align with your Master Self to activate your healing energy. Read slowly, imagining what is being described. Take the time to visualize and feel. Open yourself to receive the flow of heavenly, healing energy. Savor this experience, and come back to make this journey often.

ANGELS ARE WITH YOU

Angels are here for you, *always*. You are never alone. You are not forgotten or abandoned. You are deeply loved and treasured.

What do you need help with? The Healing Clinic is *open*!

Walk in. Bring your troubles, fears, and dis-ease. The Healing Angels are waiting for you. What do you need help with? Breathe and take a moment to feel your body. What is lacking ease, alignment, joy, or comfort? Are you emotionally challenged with a conflict? Are you suffering with sadness, grief, depression, or anger? Do recurring thoughts of self-criticism or blame torture you? Is there a situation in life that needs your attention?

Whatever it is, let it come up for healing. Focus on the most important topic and hold it lightly in your heart. Simply allow it to be present. There is nothing you need to know or do because you are in the embrace of angels.

This Healing Clinic is within the Temples of Healing, just like a walk-in health clinic may be next to a hospital. There are many Temples of Healing. Each is unique for its purpose, breathtakingly beautiful, well staffed, and abundantly supplied. Your angels transport you to the temple that best supports your need.

JOURNEY INTO ARCHANGEL RAPHAEL'S HEALING CLINIC

As you walk in, the peacefulness is astonishing! It's like a sci-fi movie where the character goes through a doorway from one world and finds herself in another.

The most immediate surprise is what is missing. Noise! There is a reverent silence. Rather than hear, you feel the harmonious vibration of the softest music. The music emanates from all around you, instantly soothing body, mind, and soul. The music itself has a sacred richness and depth that you haven't experienced in earthly music. It's as if your whole being is singing along with this ancient song of love. In a breath, you feel at peace. Safe.

As you relax into serenity, you begin to look around. The reception area is breathtakingly beautiful. There is no desk to check in, no forms to fill out, no signs, no hand sanitizer, no face masks or gloves, no wheelchairs, no chairs, no waiting!

The room itself feels alive with energy and love. The walls emit a soft glow, lighting the room. The floor is warm and radiant. You feel welcome, like coming home to a sacred place that some deep part of you has yearned for through all eternity.

ANGEL OF COMFORT

You are expected. An Angel of Comfort meets you and wraps her arms of love around you. She caresses your back, and any anxiety or fear or concern instantly melts away. There is only peace, comfort, and love. You relax like a child in the Holy Mother's embrace. Your heart knows this place of deep love. Your soul remembers sinking into eternal peace. Instantly, all is well as you are transported within your Self to the higher truth. All *is* well.

THE HEALING ROOM

The Comfort Angel escorts you to the healing room that has been meticulously prepared for you. It is so beautiful that you weep tears of gratitude as you release the burden you have been carrying. You may not even know it is there until you feel it drop away. This room contains everything you need, and it is yours to take away. Nothing is lacking. It's more like a combination museum/treasure vault than a treatment room.

Your angel motions for you to lie down. The bed is so inviting and comfortable that you sink into it. You feel as if you are floating in a universe of pure love and peace. As you venture far beyond the confines of your human body in an expansion of consciousness, all cares and worries melt away. You dissolve into this experience of unconditional love and eternal peace. There is nothing else.

One by one, loving and radiant beings enter the room. They gently surround you to lay their hands on your body in the areas that are out of balance or experiencing dis-ease.

LIGHT BEINGS TRANSMIT HEALING ENERGY

Through the hands of light beings, you feel a transmission of energy that is alive and pulsing with health, vibrancy, balance; with ease; with love and joy; with peace, pleasure, sweetness, strength, courage, ecstasy, bliss, empowerment, and possibility. Deeply receive this benediction directly from the Source.

Intuitively, you know that you are being energetically aligned with the fullness and truth of your Master Self. In truth, *you* are equally as radiant, powerful, loving, compassionate, and wise as the beings surrounding you.

You are Home. The light beings are simply helping you remember who you are. In this experience of oneness and connection, everything that is unlike this beauty, this peace, this truth is transfigured instantly into more love. The energy in your life that is contrary to this experience of bliss, this wholeness, is reconfigured. This energy is rearranged into the substance that you need to fulfill your soul calling. This divine substance is now part of your treasure vault to be used, for it is a blessing.

Your consciousness is restored as you experience oneness with your Master Self. Your body is rejuvenated as you release the imbalance of misconceptions and dis-ease. Your emotions are renewed to the full range of expression, properly perceived. Your life is reshaped to support your soul calling with everything needed. You are filled with gratitude for this experience of your Master Self and Home.

All *is* well. Invite the energy of love and peace to infuse every cell and atom in your body. Imagine your DNA being reconfigured to its pattern of perfection, instantly eliminating all physical challenges and restoring wholeness, function, and beauty to your precious body temple.

All is well. Enjoy this presence of divine love and eternal peace.

LIGHTING YOUR RETURN

Your personal healing angel remains here, lighting the way back. This is your lifeline to easily and quickly return here.

You don't want to leave this feeling or connection with the light beings that cradle you in love. You don't want to leave this experience of Home. There is no hurry, no time limit, no time! You may linger here as long as you wish. How can you leave the heavenly realm of divine love and eternal peace to return to your life? Relax. Be at peace. Know that you are loved, supported, and cared for always.

ACTIVATE YOUR DIVINITY

You have been given a reminder of your Master Self and your true Home. This activation of your divinity is meant to inspire and motivate you to do what is needed in your human life to return here often for renewal and direction. You are invited to come here daily.

As the energy immersion completes, you are provided with a plan. You feel it intuitively in your heart. This is a prescription for what to do in your earth life to heal, to resolve problems, to make better choices, to align your Master Self with your life so you may dwell in divine love and eternal peace always, no matter where you are in material creation.

You are invited to walk among the light beings. You are called upon to share your gifts and wisdom as you serve others in the same way that you have been loved and cared for here. You are being taught to live in this world and in a state of oneness with your Master Self.

YOU ARE THE BLESSING

All is well. You are loved. You are the treasure and the blessing. Knowing that your angels are here, *always*, you feel fortified and ready to return to your Earth Angel life.

To come back to the Healing Clinic, close your eyes and take a breath. Place a hand on your chest and breathe into the love in your heart to instantly be transported here by your Master Self. Return over and over to this experience of communion, of holiness, of oneness. Return often to this place of sweetness and joy, of strength and power. Breathe and be filled with this energy. Savor it. Become it; it is you.

MERGE YOUR HEALING AND MATERIAL ROOM

Come back very slowly, staying in your healing room as you become aware of your surroundings. Visualize your healing room superimposed within your physical room. Imagine the light beings, the resources, the loving energy and wisdom, simultaneously existing in your physical room so that you can access the substance and support that was provided for you. Merge your divine experience with your physical reality.

Imagine yourself with everything that you need in life: perfect health, alignment, and well-being. Peaceful, loving, and

supportive relationships. Abundance and joy, fulfillment and satisfaction. Deeply profound and intimately loving. Creative expression. Everything you need is here, now. You are completely supported in life.

Slowly open your eyes, staying in this place. Allow yourself to have the experience of being in both realms at once—both in your sacred healing room and present in your life. They coexist. You may choose which to access at any moment. You can take a breath and be in your healing room with everything you need. Your healing room is in your home! Imagine accessing your healing assets from the room you are in now. Feel the energy of the substance that has been provided for you right now, in your material room. Call it forth to manifest in your life.

Claim it as so, now.

ALIGN WITH YOUR MASTER SELF

At this higher realm of consciousness, you don't need to heal anything. There is nothing wrong. This is the most extraordinary feature of Archangel Raphael's Healing Clinic. Your body is vibrantly healthy. All you need to do is align yourself with wholeness. Call perfection into your physical body and then draw it into your life. Through aligning with your optimal pattern, you can instantly experience miracles of transfiguration and healing. Simply allow yourself to be in this presence of wholeness, completeness, abundance, and love. This is *Angel Healing!*

Everything you walked in with has been transformed. It has been transfigured into wholeness, joy, love, and connection. Everything you need right now in your life is provided. You feel fully satisfied. Let it exist in your imagination, in your heart, in your knowing, and most of all, in your energy field.

ACTIVATE YOUR ENERGY FIELD

You are experiencing *Angel Healing*. Your energy field is being activated at this moment to be a radiant, magnetic force drawing to you the demonstration of divine joy, health, abundance, love and comfort, support, everything you need. Let it be so right now in your energy field, whole and complete, already manifest. There is nothing to do.

Be aware of your magnetic energy field expanding to fill your room, while simultaneously connecting with your healing room, as they coexist. You can access both at the same time. Broadcast this presence out into your life, filling your home, your neighborhood, workplace, city, county, and your state, your country, your hemisphere, the planet! Out into our solar system, the Milky Way galaxy, out into the universe, all the way to the source of divine love. Into infinite expansion and glory in eternity. *You!* The radiant you. The Master Self you, whole and complete in the loving power and presence of eternity.

Coming back, imagine the magnificent you returning from the heavens to our universe, to the Milky Way galaxy and our arm on the spiral where our tiny solar system is, to our beautiful blue planet, back into your room, your body, and your life.

Nothing will be the same. Know that your life has been completely changed by this experience. Close your eyes and breathe yourself back into your body and life.

Know that you can return to this experience of oneness at any moment. Practice it now. Inhale into your Master Self surrounded by beautiful beings of light that love you, care for you, and nourish you in all ways. Exhale into your physical body. You are both Master Self and Earth Angel, simultaneously.

You are the precious treasure.
You are the blessing.

Experience this meditation with Kimberly at *www .AngelHealingFirstAid.com.*

2.

RECEIVE DIVINE INTERVENTION

Angels, I ask for your help. There are forces at work in my life that I cannot identify. There are blessings within my grasp if I could only recognize them. Fill me with your love that my awareness may be lifted and I may realize the true nature of these events to receive their blessings.

Recognizing your angels and how they guide you is one of the greatest blessings. *The angels offer a treasure trove of love, healing, guidance, and resources they want to pour into your heart.* As you become conscious of their presence, amazing things begin to happen. A blessing is an "infusion of holiness." When you are touched by love or peace or joy, you are blessed or infused with holiness.

Seeking divine intervention is the key to the *First Gateway Initiation.* According to Judith Larkin Reno, my lifelong friend and mentor, a *gateway* is a level of consciousness that gives us access to higher energies so we can receive divine intervention. Your soul is calling you into unitive experiences with Spirit, and Inspiration Angels are guiding you. Fortunata guides you to prosperity. Iofiel reveals your inner beauty. Israfel pops songs into your head as messages of comfort. Amarushaya helps you recognize blessings. Every angel experience brings you closer to life solutions.

There are many ways we can be blessed. Our angels communicate with us through signs and symbols. Many people tell me that they talk with their angels but don't receive a response. Angels are responding all the time. Are you ready to learn the secret code so you can easily recognize their blessing?

INSPIRATION ANGELS

Seeing a feather is a sign of grace as the angels bless you. Acknowledging this presence allows you to connect energetically. Angel Amarushaya said, "My gift is in recognizing the many forms of *blessings* in one's life. The obvious ones and the hidden blessings." Her touch softly awakens you to hidden blessings. Often, these lessons come in the form of unpleasant exchanges with family and friends. Her blessing carries the power to heal and enlighten.

Do pennies just appear? Pennies confirm that you are guided and provided for. Angels are in a natural state of abundance, as is your Master Self. Shortage doesn't exist in the heavenly realms. When you find a penny,

Fortunata, the Prosperity Angel, is saying, "Hey! You have gifts others need! Share them like this!"

Did you know angels communicate through songs? Music is a part of everything celestial. Angels sing praises. Love and joy vibrate the music of the spheres. That makes music a natural for angel communications. Angel Israfel uses music to touch your heart with messages of love, comfort, and understanding.

Do you smell roses when none are visible? Angels live in a state of beauty that is visceral. Their presence is so exquisite that it exudes fragrance, sound, and vibrations that express their state of being. Smelling scents that have no visible source is a sign that angels are with you. Angel Iofiel encourages you to sense your inner beauty and the vibrancy of your Master Self.

Once you've made the connection, the angels go before you preparing the way for a loving, abundant, creative, and fulfilling life of joy. Want to know more about the ways angels communicate? Get your free download from *www.Recognize YourAngels.com.*

ANGEL PRESCRIPTION: LIVE VIBRANTLY AND POWERFULLY

Be alert for intuitive knowing and synchronistic experiences with the following actions:

- **Identify** your need or desire for divine intervention and write about it in your journal. Go to Archangel Raphael's Healing Clinic to unify and gather resources.
- **Look for synchronicity.** While you are going about your life, watch for new connections and opportunities. Take action.
- **Share your gifts!** What gifts have you been holding back? When you need money, there is a gift inside you that is yearning to be expressed. The need for money is catalyzing your ability to share your gift.
- **Exercise** every day. Walk in nature. Move. Dance! Get your energy flowing so you are open to receive.
- **Celebrate beauty.** Dress and feel beautiful. Seek beauty around you and absorb its energy.
- **Listen** within for messages from your angels and write them in your journal. That includes intuitive knowing and visions, or guidance.
- **Take inspired action!** Follow up on your intuitive knowing and just do it!

ANGEL BLESSING: SIMPLY BE, FROM A PLACE OF FULLNESS

Simply be.
Without effort, without pretense.

Simply be, from a place of fullness.
Allow that to pour over into everything you do.

Begin with the fullness.
The illusion would have you believe that you are not full of the essence that made you. That is a lie.

You are full of the Spirit of God.
You are connected to your
Eternal Spirit.
You are a vessel of unconditional love.
You are a messenger of God.
You are a beautiful spirit of healing transformation.
You are a gift to this world.

You are the Beloved, the
Blessed One.
Feel this truth today and take action!

3.

HOW CAN I DEVELOP MY CONNECTION WITH ANGELS?

Angels, help me to experience Oneness with you today! Help me to feel your presence and recognize your assistance.

Your angels say, "We are here." *You are awakening to your Earth Angel Self and the presence of your team of angels who are with you always.* The deeper desire to feel loved, supported, and nurtured is the key to the *Second Gateway Initiation.* You are shifting from the Fourth Realm of intuitive knowing to the Fifth Realm of soul guidance where your angels reside. As I wrote in *Angel Love Cards*, "Feeling disconnected means you are unaware of your connection to your soul and to the source. The Angel of Connection is ready to help you find greater awareness."

CONNECTION ANGELS

The Connection Angel shows you how to access your Soul Star, the gateway to the angels and the closest access point to the heavenly realms. It shines etherically in your aura, just a few feet above your head. Elevating your energy body into your Soul Star opens the gateway for unitive experiences with angels.

At the divine moment of Soul Star activation, your Guardian Angel calls forth your angel team to guide your awakening. Archangel Gabriel directs pure transcendental light to flow down from the Heavens, through your soul and Soul Star, and into your body and life. Your path is illumined. An activated Soul Star makes resources of love, joy, guidance, and healing accessible to you. It's as if you can see the lock in the door. So what is the key?

Love.

As your heart chakra expands and the love that you carry becomes a palpable force in your body and life, you gain the inner strength necessary for the next escalation of Light. The Soul Star expands to reveal the lock; the love in your heart becomes the key that opens the gateway to your soul.

The angels are here!

You are granted access to the heavenly realms of existence. The soul is your first remembrance of a realm where there is only love. There is no fear or pain, no anger or betrayal, no longing or need here. The soul is the treasure vault of all goodness and supply.

Everything needed is here, waiting for you to access and retrieve for use in life, fulfilling your soul calling.

ANGEL PRESCRIPTION: ARCHANGEL GABRIEL ACTIVATES YOUR SOUL STAR

- **Breathe.** With a hand over your heart, breathe into the love that is already there. Your Guardian Angel is by your right shoulder lifting you into the presence of divine love. Can you feel it?
- **Hum** to feel the vibration of love resonate in your chest as you breathe. Change the pitch of the hum until you feel the vibration elevate from your heart to your forehead or third eye chakra. Can you feel the vibration inside your head? Archangel Gabriel is by your left shoulder opening your Soul Star and crown.
- **Look up!** With your third eye vibrating, look up in your inner vision for the Soul Star's twinkle of light above your head. Focus on the tiny light and breathe into it. Imagine it glowing brightly, expanding to hold the radiant beauty of your soul.
- **Embrace your Soul Star.** Archangel Gabriel activates your Soul Star to become a shining beacon of guidance, resources, and energy to empower your soul calling.

- **Receive.** Place a hand on top of your head. Breathe. Can you feel your crown chakra opening to connect with your Soul Star? Pure transcendental light flows down from the heavens through the Soul Star and into your physical body and world. As the wisdom and resources enter your nervous system and brain, your cellular structure and DNA are "altared." Your body is your living altar, your expression of devotion, love, and service in this world.
- **Trust** as this transfiguration takes place in the cells of your body.
- **Ask** for what you need and want. Ask to strengthen qualities of your soul. Ask for the vision of your next steps.

Want to know more? Visit *www.ArchangelGabrielSoulStar.info*.

THE LITTLE BOOK OF ANGEL HEALING

ANGEL BLESSING: THE SOUL STAR GATEWAY IS OPEN

Archangel Gabriel wants you to know that:

> Everything you need for your soul calling is here, now. Search for the place within that lives in this truth. Know that you are the Presence and Power of Divinity acting in this world. You are the hands and heart of God healing and loving people. You are the voice of Spirit bringing messages of truth and inspiration from the heavens. You are the eyes of God seeing love in everyone. You are empowered to manifest your soul calling now!

> Divine Light shines brightly upon you, illuminating your true Being. Awakening the rapture of divine love in the cells of your body. Filling the vessel of your body with energy, ideas, vision, and courage to take the leap of faith as you follow the clear guidance you receive.

> The universe is conspiring to support you with everything needed, when it is needed.

> The Soul Star gateway is open. Your activation is complete. Step through.

> We are here for you!

4.

HELP ME CHANGE!

*I'm going through a transformation and growth process.
I'm in a tough place where I'm looking at the areas of
my life that are not working. How can I gain clarity to
make the best decisions?*

Take comfort in knowing this is a magical turning point in
your life. Give top priority to your emergence into your Master
Self. *The Change Angels are activating your divinity.* Paschar is
opening your inner vision. Transcendence Angels help you rise
above the pain of loss. Action Angels support inspired change.

You are in the *Third Gateway Initiation* described by
Judith Larkin Reno, transcending soul limitations on the Fifth
Realm to experience the Sixth Realm of Divine Connection.
Your Master Self is incarnating into your life to guide your personality. Once you become aware of an area of life that needs
to change, your Master Self is signaling that you are ready to
let go and claim more conscious awareness. Your angels stand
by with your divine blueprint for the life you seek.

CHANGE ANGELS

Is fear stopping you? The Change Angel grasps your arm and leads you forward saying, "Don't look back. Don't fixate on what you are losing or leaving behind. Turn your attention to where you are going and what you are gaining."

What have you done to give yourself the message that you are letting go of the past and changing? My friend Ani Patik talked about going from Desire to Decision to Demonstration. First, you have the desire. At some point you make decisions to support that desire. Once you make an important decision that will lead to change and manifestation, immediately demonstrate it to yourself and the world.

Where are you going? Angel Paschar opens your inner senses to divine vision. Debbie Ford said in her book, *The Right Questions: Ten Essential Questions to Guide You to an Extraordinary Life:* "A conscious choice reflects our highest commitments and is in direct alignment with our vision for our lives. When we make conscious choices, we take into consideration the effect that our actions will have on our lives as a whole. We take the time to reflect on where our choices will lead us and the impact they will have on our future."

The Transcendence Angel helps you rise above agonizing loss by using pain as a catalyst to greater truth and love. Shift your focus from devastation to appreciation. What gifts are you receiving from this experience?

The Action Angel guides you to specific actions that support change based on the awareness and realizations you receive during contemplation, prayer, and meditation. Go from decision to demonstration by taking inspired action.

ANGEL PRESCRIPTION: THE FOUR STEPS MEDITATION

- **Step 1: Gain awareness.** Take gentle, deep breaths. Relax. As you breathe, notice how you are feeling. Tune in to your body sensations. What emotions come up? What are you thinking? Be present. Don't censure or judge; instead, witness thoughts and feelings with acceptance. What do you need and want? What is blocking you from that? How is this connected to the change that is happening in your life? Journal about your experience and realizations.

- **Step 2: Cherish change.** Are you ready, willing, and able to change? Invite the angels to escort you into the heavenly realm where your Master Self and soul vision await your exploration.

- **Step 3: Be receptive.** What do you feel and sense? What is your body telling you? Are you receiving guidance through angel messages or intuitive knowing? Do you see a vision of what is possible? Journal about your experience and insight.

- **Step 4: Take action.** As answers come, take action. You may receive one little step at a time. Do it. Then look for the next. Each action opens the way for more clarity and inspiration.

Want more help clearing blocks? Visit *www .ClearingBlocksToReceiving.info*.

ANGEL BLESSING: THIRD GATEWAY INITIATION

Trust.

We are here, guiding every thought and action.

Through the eyes of your Master Self, all is in divine order.

Trust. Breathe. Relax.

The Third Gateway Initiation challenges the fabric of your being to shed limitation.

You are far more magnificent than you can imagine.

Your capacity to receive and share unconditional love solves every challenge.

Your access to divine wisdom is a guiding star for humanity.

With each breath, open to the flow of higher energy.

Recognize the presence of your soul and angels.

We are here guiding you always.

You ARE the Blessing.

THE LITTLE BOOK OF ANGEL HEALING

5.

My Life Is
Falling Apart!

*I feel like I've lost everything! Job, home, family, health,
financial security. . . . Help me let go and rebuild a
new life of loving abundance.*

Everyone passes through dark nights of the soul. From the
angels' perspective, the deep pain and challenging life situations are precious times, grinding down the illusion that
covers your soul. Areas of life that are out of alignment with
your soul's calling are painfully exposed. The life you knew
crumbles.

Such challenges call you to make important life decisions.
Choices made from fear can be disastrous, like jumping from
the frying pan into the fire. Or, as you restructure your life,
*you can make decisions that lead to deeper peace, more satisfying
relationships, and greater alignment with your soul calling.*

You are in dissolution, the *Fourth Gateway Initiation.*
You are witnessing the transient, insubstantial nature of reality. Good news! Your identity is expanding to access infinite
power, intelligence, healing, resources, and divine supply.

"THE DECIDER" ANGELS

Find *hope!* Angel Phanuel never leaves your side while your worst pain is being revealed. Simultaneously, Phanuel provides opportunities to develop new relationships with angels and your soul that are deeper, more profound, and more real than you had before.

THE LITTLE BOOK OF ANGEL HEALING

Archangel Uriel said in *A-HA! A unique self-help guide to Archangel-Healing Activation Sessions,* "It is I who respond with my legions of angels when you cry out for help. We watch over you, patiently waiting for those moments of desperation when you reach out for us. That is how it is in the beginning of our relationship. As you awaken to feel the calling of your soul into the service of God, it is I who responds, guiding you to become an Angel on Call. An Earth Angel. You are literally an Angel. There is a divine plan operating in your life. I work closely with your soul, your guardian angel, and your team of angels. We are helping you to awaken to the truth of who you are. You are a great and glorious Being of Light!"

Let the urgency of pain drive you deep within, seeking a new connection with the Divine. Angel Stamera comforts you as you *forgive* the past. Let go of all that has happened. Hamied, the Angel of Miracles, is revealing your new life through synchronicity.

When you emerge on the other side in profound connection, the way is made clear. Divine love shines through your eyes. Compassion is forged in the fires of suffering. Love blossoms from the desert of despair. Empowerment arrives from the rage of injustice. New hope fills your soul and guides your life choices.

You are maturing spiritually during dark nights. Angel Paschar guides you into soul consciousness and divine intelligence as you envision your abundant new life, in alignment with your heart and soul calling.

ANGEL PRESCRIPTION: BE "THE DECIDER" FOR YOUR NEW LIFE

You have permission to be the central focus of your new life.

- **Gain clarity** about your situation. What is true? What is story? Journal daily. Write about the changes and choices that are before you each day. Explore your feelings and deeper desires. Unravel the components of your challenge so you can see the situation, your emotions, thoughts, opportunities, and outside influences clearly.
- **Envision** a life of loving purpose. What do you want? Focus on the big picture! Practicality doesn't matter here. If you had abundant resources and support, how would you set up your new life? Who would be in it? What would you do? Journey to Archangel Raphael's Healing Clinic to be guided by your Master Self.

- **Align every decision.** The little decisions matter! Each day, review your vision. Decide on the little things that bring you closer to your vision. And the big things, too. Continue to journal about your daily experiences and how your decisions are bringing you greater abundance, happiness, peace, contentment, and satisfaction.
- **Meditate on strengths.** What are your strengths? Remember a time—a body memory—when you felt strong and you did something physical that was a victory. Feel the strength in your body. Let this memory of strength carry you forward during the day as you move through changes and make decisions.

Remember, you are a great and glorious Being of Light! Shine Brightly!

ANGEL BLESSING: PRAYER TO ACCEPT ANGELIC ASSISTANCE

My beloved Angels,
Please help me to stop resisting your help.
Help me to completely trust you.
What if I could let you move me without needing to
figure out why or where beforehand?
I am so stuck in wanting to know!
This is only because I am afraid.
What a relief it would be to not have to know
everything.
Such freedom in not having to figure it out!
Help me to simply receive your hints with gratitude
and take action on them.

—Kimberly Marooney from *Your Guardian
Angel in a Box*

6.

HELP ME TO HEAL MY HEALTH CHALLENGES

I'm facing overwhelming health challenges. How can I call upon my angels to heal?

The Healing Angels led by Archangel Raphael guide you to recognize your healing gifts, to feel the sweetness of divine love, to realize old beliefs or thought patterns that contribute to illness, and to forgive past and present to allow for a restoration of health. *Healing means becoming whole.*

I suffered serious health challenges for many years. My spiritual teacher told me, "You are on the path of the body." I struggled against this concept for many years, going from one doctor to the next in search of the diagnosis and cure that could restore my health. I felt angry with my body for causing so much pain and disability. I obsessed about everything that was wrong. Eventually, I felt helpless and hopeless. All I could think about was pain and suffering.

Something magically shifted in my thoughts one day as I lay on the couch in such deep pain and despair that I wanted to die. "Lord, I don't care what happens to this body. All that matters is that I feel your love holding me now."

This prayer changed everything!

Every aspect of my being was aligned with this soulful desire to experience divine love. The full power and authority of my Being called for love *now*. I was instantly infused with ecstatic divine love that released the pain. Millions of angels surrounded me with love. Everything else fell away. There was only the loving caress of the heavenly host of angels holding me tenderly and sweetly. The past was instantly forgiven. I recognized my healing gifts and power. This was a permanent and irreversible shift. It was the *Fifth Gateway Initiation* anchoring Source and beginning the conscious descent of Spirit into matter through my life.

HEALING ANGELS

Your Healing Angels are guiding you into your pivotal moment, going from victim to master creator. Archangel Raphael, the Master Healer, hears your prayers and responds by activating your divine self and healing gifts. In the presence of your divine self, you are restored to wholeness. Daily, visit Raphael's Healing Clinic.

Serious illness gives us the time to explore our past for causes. When pain motivates you to forgive, Angel Stamera is on the scene. Stamera teaches you to recognize past experiences and people who contribute to old beliefs and repetitive thoughts that perpetuate dis-ease, and then *forgive.*

Best of all, illness has the potential to become a powerful force for awakening and spiritual initiation. When we use our symptoms to recognize where we feel disconnected, powerless, hopeless, and angry with body and life, we are ready to embrace the initiation of Enlightenment. We enlighten places that have been closed to love. The path of the body is powerful because the motivation from pain and suffering is so strong. Count yourself blessed! Realization Angels elevate your consciousness so you can see the precious opportunities being presented through the eyes of your Master Self.

True healing results when you recognize that separation from love is the source of your illness. Surrendering to loving oneness with the Divine is the cure. The Sweetness Angels hold you in bliss of divine love bringing comfort and easing pain. Gifts Angels guide you into experiences of your healing gifts and powers so you can become the healer that you are!

ANGEL PRESCRIPTION: ARCHANGEL RAPHAEL'S HEALER'S HEART AND HANDS ACTIVATION

- **Place the palms of your hands together** and hold them in front of your heart.
- **Breathe in** and release. Take another deep breath of divine love. Healing love.
- **Blow between the palms of your hands** as you exhale. Can you feel the warm Breath of God awakening the healing points in your hands? Can you feel the tremor of peace pass through your body? Raphael is *activating points* in your hands, forming a channel of healing energy from your heart to your hands. Raphael is awakening your healing gifts to heal you and others.
- **Allow** your hands to become radiant tools for Raphael's healing energy to flow through.
- **Feel** this energy. It is very subtle. Relax. Allow the tingle of energy to be there.
- **Embrace** the sense of openness and peace.
- **Place your hands** on your heart or the place in your body that needs healing.
- **Receive** healing now. Become whole in Raphael's Healing Clinic.

Want to know more? Visit *www.ArchangelRaphaelHealing Clinic.com.*

ANGEL BLESSING: YOU ARE MY
HEART AND HANDS

Raphael is calling you into service saying:

> I am he who cures.
> God cures through me.
> You are my heart and hands in this world.
> Most of the Children of Light
>   cannot yet see me or perceive my presence.
> So I turn to you, calling to my children who walk the
>   earth.
> Take my hand.
> Remember who you truly are.
> You have a unique calling and abilities.
> We have come to awaken your dormant
>   healing abilities and sleeping heart.
> Are you ready?

—Kimberly Marooney from *A-HA! A unique
self-help guide to Archangel-Healing
Activation Sessions*

7.

I'm Sinking into Sadness and Depression

*My life feels hopeless and helpless. I feel tired all
the time. I can't see any good options, as inspiration
left a long time ago. This pit feels dark and deep.
Pull me out.*

Despair is a pivotal symptom of your awakening. The Ascension
Angels are first to bring aid. Amitiel guides you into Truth.
Remliel dances around you, enticing you into Joy. The Angel
of Gifts asks the pivotal question, *"What goodness is possible
for you?"* Archangel Metatron's Ascension Chakra Activation
changes everything!

Metatron says, "I see you as you truly are in radiant
splendor and magnificent glory. We honor your devoted heart
and recognize the challenges you face. Each time you turn your
heart and soul to us, miracles happen. We are here always. You
are held and supported beyond imagining."

You are on the descension arc of spiritual initiation.
The *Sixth Gateway Initiation* infuses divine love into human
life. Your heart is using sadness and depression to call you

into deeply intimate experiences of divine love merged with human love. Turn to family and spiritual community. Don't suffer in silence! Your energy will return when you have adjusted the direction of your life to be in alignment with your spiritual awakening.

ASCENSION ANGELS

It may seem odd that Ramaela, the Joy Angel, is dancing around you. She and the heavenly host are joyfully celebrating your readiness for the Ascension Activation. For some, the Ascension Activation is immediately recognized. For others, it can take endeavor over time for the connection to open and blossom to the point of perception.

Be curious! Each time you feel sad or depressed, explore the inner territory of your being. Question your interpretation. Emotions are energy. What if you are receiving a powerful transmission of energy in response to your prayer, and your nervous system has cataloged it incorrectly? The nervous system goes into defense mode when surges of spiritual energy flood your system. Infusions of spiritual energy are easily misunderstood. What if Iofiel, the Angel of Beauty, is standing by your side with a hand on your back and you react with despair? This happens during our awakening!

The deeper purpose of the Ascension Chakra Activation is to help you perceive the presence of divine love. It is all around you and within you. Divine love is the air you breathe and the beat of your heart. It is the rays of sunshine and the grains of sand on the beach. Divine love enfolds you always. See it in the eyes of people. See it in the darkness. See it in all, guiding you Home.

Amitiel, the Angel of Truth, is fortifying your connection with the Halls of Wisdom. Amitiel is strengthening the presence of truth that dwells within you. The Angel of Gifts reinforces your connection with higher mind and divine consciousness so you *can* shift your thoughts from sadness to joy. In joy, your intuitive abilities expand to receive the flow of divine consciousness. Your soul, which holds the fragment of your essence, connects you with You! Your Master Self connects you directly with divine love, Source, and All-That-Is. You will never view sadness and despair the same again, for they are a massive invitation to activate your divinity!

ANGEL PRESCRIPTION: ARCHANGEL METATRON'S ASCENSION CHAKRA ACTIVATION

Use your inner senses to receive the infusion of activation energy as you follow these directions:

- **You are held** in love. Let Archangel Metatron's energy flow through your body. Let his energy fill the places that are closed and vulnerable. Let his blessings fill the places that are frustrated and confused. Metatron says, *"I am here!"*

- **Place your left hand** on the back of your head. Locate the notch at the base of your skull where the neck connects. Find the two sides of this notch with your index and second fingers, on either side of the soft spot. The activation starts here.

- **Breathe.** Relax. Let your touch on the spot be light and gentle. This is a place of vulnerability. Open to receive the flow of ascension energy from Metatron.

- **Move your hand** to the back of your skull, just above this point. Put your thumb in the notch. Breathe. Relax. Receive. Metatron is activating two points in your ascension chakra on the back of your head. These two points specifically connect with a quality of divine love that is gentle, comforting, and yet powerful. Can you sense your heart awakening with this energy?
- **Petals of your heart open** to the sun of divine love. There is more to you than your human self! Can you feel it?

Want more? Visit *www.Archangel MetatronAscensionActivation.info.*

ANGEL BLESSING: VESSEL OF LIVING TRUTH

Archangel Metatron wants you to know that:

> You are the vessel of living truth.
> You are the chalice of divine love.
> You are the cup of divine will.
> Others come to you to sip the nectar of eternal presence to awaken that presence within themselves.
> Your Ascension Activation is expanding your ability to respond to your soul calling.
> You are blessed.
> And you are the blessing to others.
> Stand tall and strong in truth.

8.

I Feel Overwhelmed by the Challenges in My Life

I can't deal with it! I can't focus or make any decisions.
I feel lost in the stress of too much!

We can't do it alone. We weren't meant to make life work without celestial support. Overwhelm and stress result when we think we have to figure out everything ourselves. The Surrender Angels invite you to *place your burdens on a silver platter and offer them up to the Divine.*

Jana Marie's mother fell and broke her neck while visiting on vacation. Her mother was unable to do anything for herself. Jana Marie was instantly in charge of her mom's twenty-four-hour care in addition to working full time, commuting, and taking care of her own family. One day, frozen in overwhelm, Jana Marie prayed to her angels for guidance. In her moment of surrender, a brilliant vision popped into her mind.

"A silver platter! Put my worries and concerns on a silver platter and hand them up to God and the angels. I heard very clearly, '*Surrender* your worries to us! We know what you need. We are here to help you.' I filled the silver platter with all my woes and surrendered. I had to trust that they would handle the details. Immediately, miracles began to occur daily, bringing everything and everyone we needed with Mom's recovery."

Jana Marie used the silver platter many times and guides others to do the same. The solutions for what seemed impossible arrived! Both their lives improved. Her mother can walk and take care of herself! This is the power of inviting celestial intervention into your life.

SURRENDER ANGELS

Your soul has called the Sacrifice Angels to carry you through a difficult time. Sacrifice often involves the deep heartbreak you endure when you give up something cherished to ensure the greater good of another.

Timothy Conway wrote in his book *Women of Power and Grace*, "Sacrifice: the 'making sacred' of all our situations through the power of an attitude that sees God in every event." When Jana Marie made sacred the time-consuming care for her mother, she could release resentment and see solutions.

Zacharael invites you to *surrender* your burdens. The Trust Angels help you to "let go and let God" deal with the situations. From here, you will be guided to solutions and best decisions. This is "participatory divinity," as Judith Larkin Reno called it. You are in the *Seventh Gateway Initiation.*

Ananchel, the Angel of Grace, carries you into your soul, where you can experience peace. Grace is in the solutions and resources that appear in response to your surrender.

ANGEL PRESCRIPTION: THE SILVER PLATTER MEDITATION

- **Journal.** Write about your situation. The action of writing your story signals your brain and nervous system to let go. Describe how you are making the situation sacred. Ask the Sacrifice Angel to guide you.
- **Focus.** What is the single most important thing, situation, decision, person, or challenge that you need to pay attention to right now?
- **Call your angel team.** Close your eyes to feel a connection with your angels. With your inner imagination, "see them" surrounding you with loving support. Allow your heart and soul to relax into that support.
- **Meditate on the silver platter.** Imagine you are holding a large silver platter. "See" your obstacles or challenges on the platter. If it's a person, imagine the mini-me of that person on the platter. If it's a situation, see the hologram of what is happening on the platter. Hold the platter with your challenge up to the angels. Say something like, *"Take this. I can't deal with it. I surrender it to you. I trust that you will take care of this for me. Thank you."*
- **Trust.** The angels have heard your request. Trust that they've got it for you. Trust that they will bring resolution and solutions. Release your burden. All is well.
- **Feel the grace.** Feel the grace of divine presence and instant relief now. Over time, you will witness miracles and solutions in your life. Some are very small and will

pass by undetected if you are not vigilant. Write in your journal about the miracles, solutions, synergy, opportunities, and possibilities that result from this surrender.

ANGEL BLESSING: ALLOW OUR MANTLE OF LOVE TO COMFORT YOU

We are here.
We are your angels.
We are truly with you always.
Every moment of eternity we are here.
You have never been abandoned.
You are never forgotten.
You are never without love.
We hold you always in our embrace of comfort, love,
    and peace.
We have so much we want to give you!
Please listen to us.
Search for our quiet presence in your heart.
Listen for our gentle guidance in your heart.
Allow our mantle of love to comfort you.
We are here.
We are with you now.
Allow us to assist you.
Listen for our words of wisdom.
Recognize the miracles happening to you every day!
Let the joy fall like gentle raindrops on your path.
Yes—we are here.
Believe!

9.

I'm Afraid All the Time!

Circumstances in my life feel threatening. Send Divine Intervention. Please protect me with courage, fortitude, and strength.

Protection Angels led by Archangel Michael are first responders! *Recognize that you are safe and protected now.* Cerviel, the Angel of Courage, teaches you how to find peace in the midst of fear. Fortitude angels restore power. Seraphim Nisroc delivers freedom from fear by making empowering choices.

Long ago, I was in an abusive relationship. That was real. One day at work, I was so afraid that I sat on the floor under my desk, shivering in terror. This danger was imagined. I needed divine intervention and real-life protection until the situation ended.

For many years after, I was afraid all the time. My fear eventually became an ally. It taught me to recognize my inner strength, live in a greater state of awareness, and surround myself with kind people who love me.

Who caused you to be so fearful? Is the situation over or ongoing? As you awaken and grow in light, the areas of life that are out of balance become intolerable. You go through gateway shifts. According to Judith Larkin Reno, the seven gateways are the developmental tasks for enlightenment and God realization. Your identity, reality, and consciousness radically change with each initiation. Greater love, freedom, and compassion always result.

Fear is a symptom that your natural repressed power is bursting to come forth. The *Third Gateway Initiation* is about claiming self-authority and personal power. Your soul is opening your eyes to an expanded sense of Self.

PROTECTION ANGELS

Archangel Michael asks you to look at your fear. Are you in danger now? Probably not. Take a breath and relax. Bring your focus to now. Michael is with you always, protecting you. Watch for signs of his presence. Angel Cerviel guides you to find courage in the midst of fear. From a consciousness perspective, you are stuck in the low vibration of fear. Accessing courage raises your frequency so you can make choices.

The Fortitude Angel restores your power. Ground the energy in your belly to the core of the earth. What if you were a radiantly powerful being? You are! Breathe into this possibility. Allow the energy in your solar plexus to expand upward to the heavens. As you connect with the Seventh Realm, the heavenly host stands by you. Can you sense your radiance and light in this company?

Angel Nisroc offers you freedom from fear by activating your Angel Powers. (You can find more details on Angel Powers in Chapter 20.) Opportunities pop up all day long to make decisions. Small choices can be just as powerful as big ones. Ground and connect with the Divine. Then ask, "Does this choice empower me or disempower me? Does it take me toward freedom and peace or into fear?" Each conscious choice moves you toward soul-aligned empowerment. The Trust Angel offers aid as you seek the support you need from friends and spiritual family to create a new life of safety and peace.

ANGEL PRESCRIPTION: FEEL SAFE AND PROTECTED MEDITATION

Rick Hanson, PhD, a neuropsychologist, specializes in helping patients feel happy. He suggests this guided imagery when you are fearful:

- **Know you are safe** right now, this moment. You may feel emotion or pain, but you are safe. There is no threat of danger now. How does that feel? Nothing is attacking you now. You have air to breathe. You are okay.

- **Feel protected.** Notice the walls around you or the sides of your car. You are in a relatively safe area. Recognize how you are protected. What makes you feel safe?

- **Who cares about you?** Does feeling cared for help you feel safe?

- **Be at peace.** Allow the sense of being safe, protected, and cared for to sink in. Relax into feeling at peace.

- **Take action.** What do you know you need to do to live a safer, more empowered life?

ANGEL BLESSING: INVOCATION OF THE ARCHANGELS

I invoke the blue light of Archangel Michael to surround
and protect me.

I ask him to bring me courage and to protect me from
negativity.

I ask that the brilliant blue energy of protection be
placed over me allowing only that which is for my
highest good.

I invoke the white light of Archangel Gabriel
to envelop me in his energy of purity and peace.

I ask that he help me to communicate from my heart,
through my words, thoughts, and feelings of light
and love.

I invoke the golden red energy of Archangel Uriel
to fill me with wisdom, clarity, and vision.

Soothe all conflict in my life and replace it with
knowledge and understanding of the bigger picture.

Help me make choices that are wisest for my personal
journey.

In closing, I invoke the green light of Archangel Raphael
to pour health and well-being into my body.

Help me to allow the healing to be received wholeheart-
edly and guide me to my own natural healing abilities.

Thank you and so it is!

—Sunny Dawn Johnston, *365 Days of Angel Prayers*

10.

I Have Issues
with Food

*I can't stop myself from either stuffing or starving. Help
me to face my pain and come into balance with food.
Nourish me.*

When Velma's grandma came to visit, she brought ice cream.
Velma doesn't remember much about her visits except the
chocolate ice cream push-ups that she brought. Ice cream
became the substitute for love and attention. All Velma could
focus on was getting the ice cream she loved.

Think back to your early childhood. How did food, or
the lack of it, influence your basic need for love and attention
in your family?

Food is meant to nourish our bodies. Our personal relationships, life-long curiosity to learn, and peak life experiences
are meant to nourish our hearts, minds, and souls. When
we binge or starve, we are missing the intent and blessing of
food. Has food become the medication to cover up emotional
trauma? Does it keep you busy so you don't feel pain? Do you

eat to fill up or fix the feelings? Do you starve away the needs? Food becomes an obsession, the center of life, and the God.

It is possible to feel good in your body. You can return to a nourishing relationship with food by inviting a higher power, angels, or Spirit to do for you what you cannot do for yourself. Velma's prayer is: "God, Spirit, please do for me what I cannot do for myself."

NOURISHING ANGELS

Food is at the core of our interaction with life and love. Raziel, the Angel of Knowledge, guides you to discover if you have poor eating habits or a food addiction. With addiction, there is a brain chemistry component. It has nothing to do with willpower. Food addiction means you can never get enough. You are never satisfied. You can't stop at a normal portion. The right information will guide you through the process of coming into balance with food. Want to know more? Go to *KaySheppard.com,* the website of Kay Sheppard, a leading expert on food addiction.

The Angel of Vulnerability is holding you in a tender embrace of comfort. When you feel vulnerable, turn to this angel instead of food. The Angel of Intimacy guides you through healing the trauma of feeling the energy of others. Sexual, emotional, and physical abuse can twist our natural state of loving connection from dangerous people to food. The Angel of Intimacy melts your heart into safe, blessed, and nurturing experiences with important people in your life.

Deepening your connection with the Divine to feel good instead of turning to food is the life-long solution. Stamera, the Angel of Forgiveness, invites you to forgive yourself and the others involved. The Angel of Worthiness teaches you to change your focus from resentments and blame to self-empowerment. You are worthy of love and health. The Angel of Fulfillment replaces the gnawing hunger that can never be satisfied by food with a deep sense of satisfaction and peace. Sweetness becomes emotional pleasure replacing sugar.

ANGEL PRESCRIPTION: NOURISH ME!

Worthiness Angels gently bring self-awareness and health with food from the higher perspective of Love, *now.* Here's how:

- **Stop.** When you find yourself thinking of food, at the pantry or refrigerator, searching for something in your bag, stop. Interrupt the pattern.
- **Breathe.** Close your eyes for a moment and breathe. Let breathing relax your body, emotions, and mind. Focus on the natural pause between your inhale and exhale.
- **Connect.** Call in the angels or God to lift you up into the heavenly realms of divine love. Search for a feeling of comfort or calm. Imagine your team of Nourishing Angels holding you in a tender embrace of love. Be at peace.
- **Redirect.** What is in your highest and best good right now? What do you really want? Imagine your angels infus-

ing you with the feeling that you crave. Imagine yourself filled up with satisfaction, fulfillment, intimacy, sweetness, joy, pleasure, love.

- **Choose again.** As you are feeling the satisfaction of inner nourishment, make the conscious choice to step away from food. The angels bring you back down into your body, grounded to earth with new qualities of fulfillment.
- **Find joy** in life. What is missing? What do you really want? Go after it! You are worthy!
- **Create your food plan.** Know the foods that trigger your eating challenges. Create a do-able, sustainable plan that feels nourishing and satisfying. Include portions and eat every four to five hours. Need help? Go to *KaySheppard.com*.

ANGEL BLESSING: SHOW ME THE WAY

Dear God, I need you right now!!!
I see emptiness.

   You see Wholeness.

      Angels, please show me the way.
I feel pain.

   You feel Peace.

      Angels, please show me the way.
I have nothing.

   You have All That Is.

      Angels, please show me the way.

—Rev. Velma Alford

11.

My Heart Is Aching
for My Soul Mate

*Open my heart and life to greater intimacy, healing,
and love.*

Do you have the notion that if only you could meet your soul
mate, life would be perfect? Love Angels provide clarity while
introducing the possibility of soul-connected intimacy, the elements of soul-mate relationships, and sexual healing for heart
and body. *Gratitude helps you recognize the love you already have.*

LOVE ANGELS

Angel Hadraniel teaches us to love ourselves first before calling
our soul mate. In the *First Gateway Initiation,* our ability to
love expands through pair bonding. Our interest in the inner
worlds attracts us to the concept of our soul mate.

Anael, the Angel of Sexuality, starts it. Do you think
about hot sex with your beloved as a quality of your soul mate?
Romantic, fiery sexual relationships deliver powerful lessons
of chakra opening to raise the kundalini energy in ecstatic
orgasms. This soul mate can bring out the worst in you and

spin you out of balance, and your relationship can end in heartache. Some soul mates are attracted to us for healing as we gain self-understanding and love.

Your journey of deep healing in body, sexuality, and heart prepare you for the kind of soul mate who brings out the best in you. After ascending to the Source, then descending with experiences of divine love, you have arrived at the *Sixth Gateway Initiation*. Yes, there is still hot sex . . . and much more. Because you have many soul mates to choose from in your large soul group, your depth of self-love and spiritual maturity attract a life partner. Soqed Hozi is the Cherubim of Partnership, guiding you to the most compatible mate. You are better together than alone. You are happier, more productive, and real together. Beyond a life partner who is supportive, your souls evolve together.

THE LITTLE BOOK OF ANGEL HEALING

The Intimacy Angel teaches you to feel secure and safe. You love your mate as is, without trying to make him or her into what you want. You are intuitively connected and know each other's thoughts and feelings. You flow together with little or no friction.

Your most compatible soul mate, with the attributes you desire, is on the way to you. Angel Ooniemme is your friend now, helping you to identify and feel gratitude for your soul family.

ANGEL PRESCRIPTION: RECOGNIZE LOVE

To prepare for your soul mate, write about these questions in your journal each evening before sleep:

- **Consider your relations.** Who loves you now? Family, friends, coworkers, neighbors who give you a feeling of being cared for? You matter to them. Is it your pets, spiritual friends, an angel or a spirit guide? You feel seen, appreciated, liked, and loved by them. Write about who loves you and how it feels to have their support in life.
- **Identify your community.** Which groups make you feel respected and recognized? Describe the cycle of giving and receiving with them.
- **Feel loved** now. What is it like to feel love from a past experience? What can you open to in life because you feel loved? Let loneliness and neediness fall away. How does unconditional love from the Source feel?

- **Love and care for others.** How do you care for others? Let envy, jealousy, and heartache fall away into a feeling of being loved and loving. Rest in love. Notice the cycle of giving and receiving at work. Do you give more than you receive? Do you receive more than you give?
- **Feel compassion.** Even when you don't agree? What does it feel like to be compassionate toward yourself? What would God's compassion feel like?
- **Focus on peace, contentment, and love.** Weave together a global sense that your needs are met, that you are content. No need to cling to anything in a relationship. You are safe, protected, at peace. You are loved, loving. Sleep knowing your soul mate is on the way.

THE LITTLE BOOK OF ANGEL HEALING

ANGEL BLESSING: PRAYER TO ARCHANGEL CHAMUEL FOR A SOUL MATE

Dear Archangel Chamuel,

I pray to you—please assist me in finding my perfect
    soul mate.

I am open to receive the love that is meant for me.

I have worked diligently to unlock my heart
    and am able to give and receive love now.

I long to have a life partner who will support and love
    me in all I do;

I also want to return this support and love.

Let me encounter my soul mate and allow peace
    to come to both of our lives the moment we meet.

I know that all healing comes through love
    so let us both continue to heal on our path together.

Let us come from a heart centered loving place,
    in trying times and happy times.

Never let us forget the feeling of joy and love, and how
    we began.

Help us to learn to grow as a couple;
    be willing to change for the betterment of our part-
    nership as a whole.

Wrap us in your beautiful pink wings
and pry away the cage that locks our hearts away.
Permit our hearts to soar and unite as they beat as one,
    filled with loving pink light.

—Rev. Vicki Snyder-Young, *365 Days of Angel Prayers*

12.

Resentment Is Eating Me Up!

Its persistent, nagging thoughts suck the life out of me, making me feel victimized. Help me to choose self-responsibility and self-empowerment.

That little voice is driving me crazy! "You didn't do this!" "You left me stuck to deal with that!" "I have to do this because you didn't!" Stop it! Then be grateful that an old habit has revealed itself for release. You are not a victim to the habits of your brain! *You are worthy of love, appreciation, and support.*

It starts like this. I ask my beloved to do something, and he doesn't. Then I feel resentful. That resentful voice gripes endlessly about what he didn't do and what it will cost me in time and energy to do it.

The neurons in your brain have receptors for emotion. Vianna Stibal said in *ThetaHealing: Introducing an Extraordinary Energy-Healing Modality,* "Once a receptor is used to an emotion, it has to have it, just like a drug. So, if you are used to being depressed, you will create depression."

Resentment fits into this category. If you have a habit of feeling resentful, your neurons are searching for opportunities to whip up resentment to feed the habit. According to Stibal, you can learn to live without resentment, helping the brain shut down the receptors that are looking for it. And you can strengthen neuron receptors to accept worthiness, appreciation, and responsibility.

APPRECIATION ANGELS

When you catch your thoughts spinning resentment, Angel Ooniemme is waving at you saying, "Hey! Have *gratitude!*" Shift your perception to something that makes you feel grateful.

Turn the tables! The Encouragement Angel is offering you a new perspective. Look for evidence of encouragement and support in life, or imagine the person you resent encouraging and supporting you! Search for the tiniest experiences as a start.

Resentment is evidence that you believe you are unworthy of support and appreciation. The Angel of Worthiness counters that belief with the truth. You are worthy of so much more! Contemplate the questions, "What goodness can I create in my life? What soul qualities are being strengthened by this experience?"

Sandalphon, the Seraphim of Power, converts the energy of resentment into empowerment. You are a powerful creator. Ground into the earth; then raise your energy to the Seventh Realm of angels like we did in Chapter 9 with the Fortitude Angel. To reprogram your brain receptors, Stibal suggests you say, "I release resentment and I understand what it feels like to live without resentment." Can you imagine how empowering that feels? Then affirm, "I know how it feels to be supported." Hang out in the feeling of support.

Galgaliel, the Angel of Vibration, helps you change the energy of the relationship from resentment to appreciation, encouragement, and love.

ANGEL PRESCRIPTION: FRESH START

- **Stop.** The moment you realize that you are overwhelmed with resentment, stop. Take a shower and wash your hair. Put on attractive, clean clothes that you don't usually wear. Change the vibration of your energy. Affirm, "I understand what it feels like to be supported."
- **Journal** about your situation. What are your resentments trying to reveal to you? What needs are not getting met? Is the person crossing your boundaries? Did you ask for what you want? Write until you gain clarity about your part in it. What do you want to receive? What do you want to feel? What is your responsibility? How can you shift your perspective and behavior to change the dynamic from resentment to empowerment?
- **Change!** Often when we feel resentful, we don't have control over the person or situation. What do you have

control of that you can change right now? Clean something in your house: change the bed sheets, do laundry, wash dishes. Or help someone else, taking the focus off yourself. Are you resentful that something isn't happening? Do it yourself! As Vianna Stibal suggests, reinforce a new thought by saying to yourself, "I know how to live without being miserable."

ANGEL BLESSING: DIVINE FORGIVENESS

Forgiveness is the next step.

> The forgiving, releasing, and healing power of God works in and through me now.
> All judgment, resentment, criticism, and unforgiveness are now dissolved and healed.
> With the love and peace of God within my heart, I forgive everyone of everything—including myself.
> I now forgive all past experiences.
> I now forgive myself for all seeming errors, mistakes, and wrongdoings.
> I bless myself. I AM forgiven. I AM free.
> Thank you God, and SO IT IS.

—Susan Shumsky, *Instant Healing*

13.

I Have Issues with Sex

*I've been abused sexually and feel afraid and guilty
having sex, even with my spouse! Help me release
the past and open to the pleasure of sensuality
and sexuality.*

The majority of us have sexual issues. For many of us, it began
in childhood with molestation and rape. Whether we shut
down in fear or became promiscuous, it's time to heal. Women
speaking up through the #MeToo movement are changing the
shocking fact that sexual abuse is accepted as normal!

*Sexual energy is a powerful and creative force, intended to
increase the light in each of us.* Our energy opens up during sex.
Sexual energy is magnetic, attracting partners who reinforce
our patterns.

GOLDEN INCARNATION ANGELS

Whether we are going after sex or avoiding it, our souls crave
intimacy. Sex doesn't bring us closer, love does. In *Angel Love
Cards*, the Intimacy Angel teaches us that, "Intimacy happens

when two hearts connect in the sincere desire to experience something new. Expectations, on the other hand, prevent intimacy." Are you willing to see into heart and soul without expectations?

Before your birth, your Guardian Angel, Master Self, and angel team had many meetings with the Kindle and Divine Plan Angels to determine the most important elements for this life. What issues will you face? What karmic debts will you resolve? Who will embody to support healing? Who will be your soul mates? What opportunities will you have? Your Golden Incarnation Disc was formed and placed in your heart with this program of blessings, challenges, and soul calling opportunities.

Sexual issues are high on the list of healing opportunities. If it feels as though you have worked on your sexual issues forever and they keep coming back, you are right. The *First Gateway Initiation* takes you through sexual issues, and then you come back to them as you awaken.

Good news! Your Golden Incarnation Disc is being upgraded, programming in a much larger potential for healing and accomplishment. You can go beyond the karma and beliefs that captured you in sexual issues. Angel Anael is revealing how to heal and transform into pleasurable experiences of sexuality. Release the past, forgive, accept, and transcend. The Sensuality Angel is offering opportunities for profound exchanges of intimacy and love. The essence of your world is being reconfigured to include sensuality and orgasmic delight.

Welcome to the *Sixth Gateway Initiation* of intimacy and unconditional love. Your Master Self is descending from Source to bless you. By seeing the face of God in the people in your life, you may discover a committed love relationship and even a new marriage with a partner who matches your soul.

ANGEL PRESCRIPTION: SPEAK UP!

- **Use discernment.** Are you safe with your lover? If not, get guidance from a professional. For healing, you need a sexual partner who is trustworthy, loving, and willing to help you through your fear and pain.
- **Be honest** about your feelings first with yourself, and then include your partner. Love is a feeling in your heart. Are you holding back for fear of rejection? Say that! Talk about your history.

- **Try new things.** Tell your lover what you want. Be adventurous. If you are afraid, say it. If you feel ashamed, say it! Healing begins with the intention to end denial.
- **Go slow.** Be sensitive to your smallest fears or desires. Perceive your thoughts and feelings as guides to healing, rather than tormentors. At first, you may only be able to cry as you begin to release deep pain. Acknowledge it. Talk!
- **Love heals.** In the presence of self-love, honor your feelings to reclaim your power. Speak up! Do you feel guilty about your sexuality? Are you ashamed of past behavior? Are you angry? Quit lying to yourself and become aware of what happened to you and how you really feel.
- **Love your body.** As you clear out past history and your energy opens, let your body become your beloved friend. Let it tell you what it wants.
- **Be sensitive** to your partner's needs and conscious of your motives. This sensitivity goes two ways.

ANGEL BLESSING: REWRITE YOUR GOLDEN INCARNATION DISC

Fill your heart with love and joy.

Leave behind endless processing and waiting.

Leave behind recurrent patterns and beliefs you haven't been able to shake.

Leave behind fear and worry, doubt and questioning.

Your Master Self is here offering full alignment.

Simply breathe and relax in wholeness, completion of Being, infinite wisdom, and abundance.

There is nothing to do or figure out.

No effort or struggle, only love and grace.

Let your heart be filled with love and grace.

You have exceeded the highest expectations of the heavens for what was thought possible when you were born!

Your Golden Incarnation Disc is upgraded to increase what is possible.

Your Master Self brings forth wisdom and guidance, abundance and all-sufficiency.

Your Master Self is upgrading your physical body, cells, atoms, systems, energy bodies, and chakra systems, even your soul contract!

You are in a state of limitless possibility, opportunity, unconditional love, and joy.
Go beyond limited thinking as you are literally transfigured into the Master Self that you have always been.

As you ascend into planetary mastery,
simultaneously descend into a life of greater love.
Welcome to the Sixth Gateway Initiation blessing of intimacy and unconditional love.

14.

I'VE LOST SOMEONE I LOVE
AND GRIEF IS DEVASTATING

*I can barely think or function. My life feels empty. I not
only lost my beloved, but I also lost who I think I am.
Show me the light.*

Your Guardian Angel leads this team of Comfort Angels, helping you reconnect with the fullness of your Self. Immersion
Angels fill you with sweet, comforting peace and love. An
angel message brings peace.

Grief reminds us that we have agreed to be limited to a
body. Collective consciousness says that when our loved ones
die, they are gone. Remember that you are an earth angel.
Remember that you are more than your body and personality.
*Remember that we are all one in divine love. You are a bridge to
spirit!*

At the *Sixth Gateway Initiation,* you have the ability to
expand your perception of self, others, and existence. Grief
brings the energy of expansion and connection when properly
perceived. The transition of your beloved is an invitation to

remember your light bodies. Remember your Master Selves. Remember your existence together in eternity.

As a bridge to spirit, your soul embodied with the purpose of shining light into the darkness of forgetfulness. You and your beloved agreed that this time of transition signals the revelation that we are not separate. Now is the time for your expansion into the full realization of your Master Selves and beyond, into All-That-Is. Your beloved is leading the way.

What if this time of transition could become ecstatic union with your beloved in eternal love? Breathe this in! Feel its potential. With each breath, expand into the embrace of Home. This is the *Seventh Gateway Initiation!*

THE LITTLE BOOK OF ANGEL HEALING

COMFORT ANGELS

The healthy function of grief is to create space for your new identity and new life. The Comfort Angel elevates your consciousness to remember your Master Self. Excessive grieving means you are stuck in hazards of the *Fifth Gateway*. When grief compresses your heart and you feel as though you are sinking into sadness and loss, the Angel of Immersion taps on your left shoulder.

Reinterpret your feelings to deep unconditional love, drawing you into a new place within. It may feel heavy at first. We need all of the tools we can get to awaken to our Master Selves. Music is one of the most powerful. Israfel, the Angel of Music, suggests Samuel Barber's *Adagio for Strings* to help your heart steer upward.

Ooniemme, the Angel of Gratitude, invites you to remember that the Master Self of your beloved is with you always. Redirect energy of grief into gratitude for this awakening moment. The Angel of Companionship is the alchemist transforming grief into golden comfort of sweetness and peace in the eternal presence of your beloved.

Each time you feel grief, your Guardian Angel is tapping on your right shoulder saying, *"Remember. We are here."* Breathe and relax. Expand your sense of self to include the presence of your beloved and your angel team.

ANGEL PRESCRIPTION: BRIDGE TO SPIRIT MEDITATION

Based on a breath meditation received by Judith Coates in *Jeshua: The Personal Christ, Vol. IV:*

- **Breathe.** Relax. Allow your chest to expand with your breath. Feel the peace that comes with breathing.
- **Feel yourself as light.** The light of your essential self surrounds you, activating the body. Feel the soft golden light around you illuminating everything.
- **Reach out to your beloved.** Breathe again, and in your light body, allow your inner senses to extend out to your beloved.
- **Communicate with love.** Allow your inner knowing to connect with your beloved in unconditional love. No words are needed. Be at peace together in love. Be one in the light.
- **Speak from your heart.** What would your heart say to your beloved? The innermost being of you speaks to the innermost being of your beloved connecting in oneness, in communion, in love.
- **Listen.** What does your beloved say to you? Receive the message.
- **Bless** your beloved with your love. Receive the blessing of love in return. Know that you can connect and speak anytime. There are no barriers to communication and coming-into-union.

ANGEL BLESSING: CHANNELING ANANCHEL IN ALL HER GRACE

It has come to my attention that as humans you often question the beyond. I am here to tell you that what may seem to be light years away is only a whisper, and that your loved ones are not only safe, but truly happy, and filled with joy. As they look down from the heavens they still see and feel your love, and devotion, and they know how you yearn for the day when you will see them again. I am here to tell you that the day will come when you will be reunited. This will be a truly joyous occasion, and one that will connect your souls for eternity. So smile when you think of your loved ones, for each smile is seen, and each prayer is heard, as the love is felt deep within the hearts of all those who wait for you in the heavens.

—Excerpted from Rev. Cathi Burke,
Americo Michael: Surrounded by Angels

15.

I Regret Something I Did and Feel Guilty

Help me release this awful feeling of shame, let go, learn from the experience, and become a better person from it.

Your experience is your wake-up call. Learn from it, make amends, and move forward. The Transcendence Angels are here with humility, courage, forgiveness, and appreciation to cut the cords of this past and cocreate a new life of purpose.

You didn't take birth to suffer endlessly. You took embodiment for a specific purpose. *You are a unique and powerful aspect of divine love.* Your purpose is your unique way of contributing wisdom and life force to humanity. You came here to be the voice of compassion. You are here to bring peace.

Your experience was designed to make you an expert in uplifting lower vibratory energy. That is what a peacemaker does. Would you like to know what life could be like without this guilt defining you? Lift up your mind and heart to the highest, purest thought of the Divine about you. Listen to the voice of encouragement from your angels. Your mission to uplift the consciousness of humankind starts with you.

Quantum physics confirms that everything is energy. Each emotion vibrates at a specific frequency. Our feelings determine our level of consciousness. Your life now is a reflection of your past frequency. You have the power to change.

In his book *Power Vs. Force,* David Hawkins shares his insight into energy, which can help identify where you are so you can raise your energy to change your life. Hawkins calibrated the energy levels of consciousness. For example, regret is 75, guilt is 30, and shame is a low 20. Angels vibrate at over 1,000, so how can we connect? Here's where the angels come in with divine intervention.

the Little Book of Angel Healing

TRANSCENDENCE ANGELS

Angel Cerviel gives you courage to confront your past, elevating you to 200, where you are empowered to shift your concepts of self. The Humility Angel teaches you to see the best in yourself. Humility is an open state where you can receive goodness, love, and grace. Angel Stamera encourages you to take responsibility for your past actions. Forgiving yourself and others lifts your energy to 350, where the Transcendence Angel shows you how to let go. Shifting your attention from devastation to appreciation raises your frequency to 500! What gifts are you discovering from this experience? The Appreciation Angels inspire you to recreate yourself in radiant divinity.

Is your own healing enough? Or do you need to make amends with someone? Your angel team is standing strong with you as you write the letter, make that phone call, or meet in person. Humility is strength in the power of truth. You don't need approval or permission from anyone but your Self.

ANGEL PRESCRIPTION: ARCHANGEL JOPHIEL'S "THE QUICKENING" ACTIVATION

"The Quickening" raises your energy to over 1,000 and the heavenly realms!

- **Put your palms together** in front of your third eye or forehead. We are closer than your own breath and heart beat. We are One. You are a part of us, and we are a part of you. There is no separation.
- **Breathe** and feel this connection. It is visceral, physical, and much deeper. The inner senses add multidimensional presence that goes beyond the physical senses, yet they

are connected. Notice everything—even the smallest sensations. Our connection comes through the subtlest hints. When you breathe into them, they blossom and open into powerful transmissions of energy, providing guidance, healing, love, resources, abundance, everything you need in life to fulfill your soul calling.

- **Place fingertips on your forehead**, between your two eyebrows. Notice how this feels.
- **Move the skin** gently back and forth from left to right. Notice how you feel. What changes?
- **Pull down.** Pull the skin down toward your nose, a gentle, tiny movement. What shifts?
- **Make tiny circles** in a counterclockwise motion on your forehead. Notice the feelings.

- **Lift** the skin up to the left. Lift up to the right in a "V" shape.
- **Receive.** Ask to know your radiant, loving, kind, wise, and generous Master Self.

Want more? Visit *www.ArchangelJophielQuickening.info*.

ANGEL BLESSING: BELIEVING MEDITATION

There is no better time than now to believe. It is not sometime in the future when you have established yourself. When you have perfected yourself in a way you perceive as somehow better. When you have more loving relationships. It is now while you are in the midst of chaos, confusion, and doubt that belief can serve you.

You will never reach your goals if you only ponder and dream for then they are just phantoms drifting in your imagination.

Trust in your journey so that no matter what, you are always on the right path, even if it seems that rocks and boulders slow your progress. Have faith in your ability to access the Divine part of you even if at times you feel shame and guilt. Believe that you will be supported each step of the way even though you do not know where you are going or how you will get there.

So Beloved, reach out believing. Believe you can. Believe you will.

—Excerpted from Rev. Saxon Knight, *Seraphim Angels: Guide to the Healing Path of Love, Book Two*

16.

I Feel So Agitated!

Nothing I do seems to help. I can't stand it another moment! Please guide me in my search for Peace.

Feeling agitated is a symptom that your prayers are being answered. The Immersion Angel is responding with a massive influx of the spiritual energy. In *Angel Love Cards*, I wrote, "In a state of immersion, you are connected with divine intelligence so you can see the bigger picture to solve problems creatively. *Unlimited energy flows through you, allowing you to physically accomplish your purpose.* Immersion in unconditional love stimulates awareness enabling you to recognize revelations, opportunities, resources, healing, and relationships that are being provided to accomplish your purpose."

What have you been praying for?

CREATIVE POWER ANGELS

I used to suffer from anxiety. I would feel so agitated that I thought I was going to jump out of my skin. After several days of suffering, I'd get to the point where I would stomp around in my meditation room screaming, *"What! What!"* I didn't like how I felt, I didn't understand what was happening, and I didn't have any answers.

One day in a fit of screaming *"What!"* I had a profound realization that changed my life. I was misinterpreting my experience! This angel helped me understand that agitation and other emotions are energy. That's when I started to call this "Angel-Induced Agitation." I wondered, "What have I been praying about?" As I moved through agitation in this way, the realization dawned on me, "Oh, this *is* the answer to my prayers!" The Immersion Angel was infusing me with intense spiritual energy containing the resources I needed.

The nervous system receives the influx of spiritual energy through the chakras. As more energy flows into the nervous system than usual, it reacts as if it is being attacked. The first defense is anxiety and agitation.

Once I start to cooperate with the influx of energy, the guidance flows. Archangel Jophiel directs for my next steps with creative power to solve the problem. The energy shifts from being unpleasant to ecstatic union with my Master Self. Gratitude washes through me as my perception changes. Ooniemme expands the energy into more opportunities.

What if you could change your perception? Agitation can turn into ecstasy. You may feel like a joy fountain, leaping and splashing all over everyone.

ANGEL PRESCRIPTION: TRANSFORM AGITATION THROUGH MOVEMENT MEDITATION

Gather angel cards, journal, pen, water, and a variety of music. Follow this sequence:

- **Focus.** What situation in life needs your attention? What have you been praying for? Select the strongest emotional focus. Make a few notes in your journal.
- **Call your angel team.** "See them" with your inner imagination or envision them surrounding you with loving support. Let some deep part of you receive and relax into that support.
- **Move!** Put on heavy metal music, drumming, or anything powerful; then stomp around the room. Emote! Let your feelings come out. Say the words that need speaking. Scream into a pillow or towel. Don't try to manage or understand.
- **Pray!** As you move, turn whatever you are experiencing into a conversation like this: *"Angels, I hate this feeling! I hate it because I don't understand it. Change my perception so I can see the gift you are trying to give me!"*

- **Receive.** Allow your emotions to shift to empowerment, naturally. Change the music to support your new experience. Let your conversation change to *"Thank you for this intense energy in answer to my prayer. Guide me into ecstatic union with my Master Self."*
- **Fine-tune.** Imagine you are a radio receiving signals. Agitation sounds like static. Adjust the tuning knob to find joy, love, peace, courage, prosperity, and everything you need! What do you need to strengthen in yourself? Find it. Change the music to support your experience.
- **Superimpose** your experience of feeling calm, connected, supported, or provided for over your current life. Imagine the blessings this experience is bringing to your life.
- **Gain clarity on your purpose.** Once you feel naturally calm, sit. Write questions that have the potential to connect the dots in your journal, and then be open to receive responses or realizations. For example, *"How does this immersion of spiritual energy answer my prayer? I need to know how to solve a problem, or make a better decision, or feel connected with . . ."* Write what you know, sense, feel, hear, realize, understand, or see. If you have angel cards, draw one or more for greater clarity on your next steps.
- **Be grateful.** Linger in the heartfelt, full-body experience. Imagine your angel team going before you in life, preparing the way for a most amazing experience of feeling loved, guided, and supported. Journal about your experience with gratitude.

ANGEL BLESSING: SWEETNESS OF DIVINE LOVE AFFIRMATION

I don't need to feel anxious now.

I AM deeply immersed in divine love, ecstasy, peace, prosperity, abundance, and wisdom!

I take time to tune in and receive what is being provided in this moment.

I breathe in divine energy in answer to my prayer.

I breathe out gratitude and fulfillment.

Life is good.

I am grateful for everything I receive:

Realization, guidance, comfort, encouragement, EVERYTHING!

As I breathe in, I receive.

As I breathe out, gratitude flows from me.

It is the circle of life, receiving and giving.

And so it is.

17.

GET ME OFF THE ROLLER COASTER OF POVERTY!

I can't seem to shake the feast-or-famine cycle. I feel like a bottomless pit! Help me end this cycle of poverty and open to prosperity.

No matter how much I had, it was never enough. I created this scenario over and over, unable to release the pattern! Abundance Angels reveal old beliefs that perpetuate poverty of consciousness and pocket, then provide Golden Elixir for opening to abundance and miracles.

Divine intervention put *Emergence: The Shift from Ego to Essence* by Barbara Marx Hubbard into my hands. Barbara wrote, "When we follow the deficiency as deeply as possible, . . . we let our local selves discover that the fulfillment they've been seeking is already present in the Beloved."

While I'd been dancing around this knowing, I hadn't been able to experience it. As I followed Barbara's directions in a life-changing meditation, I knew that *Infinite Supply is a quality of my divine Master Self.* In the embrace of the Beloved, I feel myself becoming Infinite Supply. Beyond gaining access,

I have become Infinite Supply. Everything I need and am seeking has already been given to me through the Beloved.

Immediately after the experience, I was confused. It seemed like everything had changed, and nothing had changed. I still had the same bills and limited cash flow. An inner voice said, "Stop. Breathe. Relax into the Beloved." When I did, the Abundance Angels pulled the veil back and I saw magic!

ABUNDANCE ANGELS

Anxiety became a doorway into Infinite Supply in the embrace of my Master Self. I could see how each experience of not having enough was pointing me toward this experience of my self as the creative field. The connection between my beliefs and situation in life became clear. It wasn't a cash flow issue; it was a "me" issue. Worthiness Angels guide you to see life deficiencies as opportunities to become Infinite Supply when you feel anxious.

I could never accomplish what is being asked of me. My Beloved Self with Infinite Wisdom and Supply can! The more my Master Self lives through me, embracing the limited selves that can't possibly accomplish the tasks given them, the clearer solutions and resources become. It's true! Everything I need and am seeking has already been provided through my Beloved Self. Angel Fortunata reminds you to call forth inner prosperity when you have needs. Focus on the abundance that you have now and how it benefits others.

For the first time, I feel supported. The Master Self abides within me. I become the expression of divine essence in the world. I *am* Infinite Supply. Transcendence Angels help you to

"Stop, breathe, and turn everything into Divine Opportunity" when you forget. Fulfillment Angels guide you to create wealth by adding value to what you do so it helps your community. What do you wish to share? Keep your attention on the fact that you have it now and you want more of it to help others.

ANGEL PRESCRIPTION: GOLDEN ELIXIR

Adapted from Barbara Marx Hubbard's Diamond Approach in *Emergence: The Shift from Ego to Essence.*

- **Breathe** into your heart. Through the love in your heart, invite Divine Essence to fully inhabit you.
- **Feel the light of presence** shining on you. Can you feel its comforting embrace?
- **Be love.** Radiate the light of divine love. Radiate the inner presence of love upon the part of Self that is suffering.
- **Focus** on a deficiency.
- **Experience** the hurtful wound and memories connected with it.
- **Open** yourself to feel with no thought of how to fix it.
- **Allow** it to fully express with no judgment.
- **Invite** the Limited Self to guide you precisely to the quality that you have been seeking.
- **Be present** with the quality as Golden Elixir flows out of it, healing and filling the emptiness with a sweet fullness that melts the heart.
- **Absorb goodness**, erasing your fears and patterns.
- **Receive an infusion** of this essence until it brings you to contentment.

- **Call your angel** to be your guide, asking for the wisdom or message you need.
- **Linger** in the essence of fulfillment and Infinite Supply.

ANGEL BLESSING: ARCHANGEL CHAMUEL BE-LOVED

LOVE is the power of creation.
You are called upon to cocreate with love.
You are chosen to expand with love.
You are destined to become the great
Presence of love that you already are.
The power of divine love already flows through you.
You are composed of love, guided by love, inspired by
 love, nourished by love, motivated by love.
Love provides all things, abides all life.
It's you! You are Love.
BE in Love.
Be LOVED.
Everything in life has pointed
 you to this moment.
Invite your beliefs in limita-
 tion to lead you into Infinite
 Supply.
Your stories of "never having what
 you need" lead to resources
 waiting for you.
In truth, you command the ultimate
 authority to cocreate.
You are the BE-LOVED.

18.

I Am Not Stubborn!

I'm embarrassed to admit that my own inner movement is stagnating. I'm not taking the opportunities before me to try new techniques or to explore new ways of thinking.

My knees had been aching for weeks. I looked up knee pain in Louise Hay's book, *You Can Heal Your Life*. I had the pleasure of meeting Louise several times. She wrote, "Love Heals" when she signed this copy to me. Under "Knee Problems," Louise wrote, "Stubborn Ego and pride. Inability to bend. Fear, Inflexibility. Won't give in." My first response was, "I don't have a stubborn ego!"

That was it. My stubborn ego revealed itself instantly. The golden question was "What am I being stubborn about?" When we become curious, the issue surfaces in life saying, "Me! Me! It's this!" *When the light of awareness shines on the old pattern, it sparkles, begging to "Please! Let go!"* Even the pattern is tired of itself! Let go of the fear of doing it wrong, losing the path, or disappointing someone else.

Loyalty! It comes down to my misplaced sense of loyalty. I'm very loyal to people, beliefs, and rules that create a safety net or structure around me. If I believe this or do that, then I'm safe or connected. . . . If this, then that. Sounds like a computer program.

This way of thinking and living stops me from exploring. I don't read books, attend courses, or try new things. I'm loyal to a form of yoga or an author or master. I won't divert from an eating protocol or self-care routine. I don't venture outside the safety zone I've created for myself. That led to stubborn clinging and stagnation.

Judgment! Another component is uninformed judgment. Without knowing anything about other authors, eating styles, beliefs, or opportunities, I have a judgment that what I'm doing is superior. With this mindset, I'm not curious. I don't read or try new things. Staying loyal to my "tried-and-true" path was creating health issues, stubborn clinging, and stagnation.

Read the book! Go see the master! Try a new form of eating or yoga! Talk to a friend who has been trying to share a new interest or practice! Become curious and explore!

RESPOND-ABILITY ANGELS

When you realize that you are stuck in stubbornness, your angels escort you into a more flexible, willing, and pliant state where you have the ability to respond to life changes.

Archangel Michael protects your spiritual destiny. Stubbornness creates a twisted sense of protection that holds outdated beliefs and harmful behaviors in place. Michael guides you to literally burn away self-imposed limitations that block you from pursuing your spiritual path. Willingness and pliability result, making it possible to feel safe flowing with life changes.

The Angel of Illumination reveals the truth of stubbornness by shining the light of love upon aspects that keep you stuck. New opportunities are revealed that bring you into greater joy and expression.

The Angel of Passion guides you to see the situation from a curious and flexible perspective. What matters most to you? Have fun experimenting with new options. Jump on opportunities. Allow your passions to run wild as you recreate your life to serve your higher purpose.

Angel Charmiene introduces new people, ideas, and possibilities that bring you into harmony with your true essence.

ANGEL PRESCRIPTION: WHAT MATTERS MOST?

- **Breathe** into your heart and soul.
- **What matters most** to you?
- **What if** you had the time, money, support staff, technology, opportunity, and connections to create your biggest visions? What if there was nothing to stop you or slow you down? What if you had everything needed to change the world? What would you create? What would you do? What matters most?
- **Who matters most?** Looking at it from a darker perspective, what if the world as you know it were ending in ten years? What would be most important for you to experi-

ence or express with important people between now and then?

- **Take action.** What can you do about that *now?*

Journal about your realizations. Come back to these questions often to explore different perspectives. Notice how your stubbornness affects your ability to respond to your deepest passion. Find a way to become more flexible, pliant, and willing. Do one thing each day that moves you toward your passion.

ANGEL BLESSING: YOUR GLORIOUS SELF

You are the miracle maker.
You are the benediction.
You are the blessing and the blessing giver.

Be your Self!
Your true Self!
Your glorious Self!

Be radiant.
Be love.
Be joy.
Be abundant and prosperous.
Be at peace.

We are here.
We are with you always.
We have so much to give you!
Receive.

19.

I'm Stuck! How Can I Play Bigger in Life?

None of the old ways are working for me. Thank God and just as well! I've been pushed into a place of discomfort to receive the bigger message within: to trust and have faith, angels are with me. How can I work with my angels?

Rejoice! You are experiencing identity expansion as you enter the *Fourth Gateway Initiation.* Your old identity and ways of living dissolve so your Master Self can lead. Discomfort becomes the fertile ground of creativity. Best of all, you feel the deeper call to selfless service, playing bigger to offer more of the gifts and essential qualities of soul.

WHAT IS THE OPPORTUNITY TODAY?

When you need guidance, breathe and focus within. Angels announce themselves in the "feeling" of tingles and flutters. The tingles—the sensation of energy moving—are just that, energy moving. Your angels are increasing the flow of divine love. When you feel a spot tingling, focus on it with love. The energy of love is clearing, aligning, and balancing a "record" in that spot.

"Records" are the energy history of an experience, decision, belief, or action. By flooding a record with new love energy, the past is released. Space is open for a new record to replace it. What will your new record be? Can you hold a focus of alignment, balance, and wholeness? Can you envision a reality of abundance?

OPPORTUNITY ANGELS

Archangel Jophiel uses creative power to draw opportunity from your divine plan. What don't you like that you want to get rid of? (Discomfort of feeling disconnected from Spirit.) What do you want? (Manifest visions expanding service and Divine Presence.)

When you focus on what you don't want (disconnection), it perpetuates. When you focus on the vision of what you want (connection), it takes on form and manifests.

Archangel Metatron focuses thought. While it is helpful to understand challenges and issues so you can see them clearly, the next step is critical. Will you focus exclusively on what is wrong? Will you dedicate a lifetime to reliving the trauma? Or, are you ready for a quantum shift into the Field of Unified Creation?

Jophiel and Metatron are walking with you hand in hand, helping you walk away from old ways of perpetuating issues and suffering. When opposing thoughts pop up, acknowledge them. Approach the thought with a cozy, warm blanket and cup of hot cocoa. Wrap the blanket of comfort around the thought. Drink cocoa together. Ask, "What do you want me to know? How can I take better care of you?"

Angel Remliel advises, "Have mercy on yourself. Choose to release the past. You have served your time. All debts are paid. All karma fulfilled. You are free to go forward." Angel Zacharael asks, "Can you surrender into health? Can you surrender into love and joy? Can you surrender into more awesomeness, empowerment, glory, and magnificence than you ever before thought possible?"

What is the opportunity today? How can you breathe and rise up into the Light? Can you trust, allow, and expand? Can you receive and take action?

ANGEL PRESCRIPTION: UNIFIED FIELD OF CREATIVE POWER

- **Recognize** what needs adjustment (disconnection).
- **Focus** on creative power (manifesting bigger service and visibility through connection).
- **Remember** a time when . . . (I felt intimately connected with angels and cocreated with ease and power!).
- **Breathe** in that energy, possibility, and opportunity!
- **Metatron lifts you up** to the *Seventh Realm of Cocreativity* where the Creator resides.
- **Connect** with the divine blueprint of you—the DNA of optimal health for your body, mind, heart, spirit, and life.
- **Overlay** the blueprint on your current energy body.
- **Align** your cells to this pattern of perfection for your soul calling.
- **Allow** your body to change instantly in this pattern of perfection.
- **Breathe** in joy, vibrancy, possibility, and ecstatic action.
- **Focus** on this opportunity.

ANGEL BLESSING: BREAKING THROUGH ILLUSIONS THAT KEEP YOU SMALL

Archangel Metatron,

I call on you now to help me align with my inner truth.

Help me to call in the angels and follow my divine guidance.

I cast out all negative thoughts and break through illusions created by my ego to keep me small.

I step into this knowingness and allow the magnificence that I am to flow into and through my veins

replacing all illusions and negative thought projections with the purity and love from my soul.

As I align with God's will in my life, I am shown the way, and where there is no way, miracles unfold and the path is revealed.

Illusions that served me once are now disintegrating and fading from my sight.

My essence is as pure and sacred as a newborn child and as I tap into this truth, there is nothing that I cannot be, do or have.

Only love exists now. Only love.

Thank you, Archangel Metatron, for helping me to remember who I am and why I came here.

By the grace of God it is so.

Thank you. Thank you. Thank you.

—By Julie Geigle, *365 Days of Angel Prayers*

20.

How Can I Express
My Soul Purpose?

*I'm questioning how I can be of greater service, benefit,
and value to my Divine Source. I want to be in a position to help people, satisfying my divine plan.*

You are a unique and powerful aspect of divine love and eternal truth. Your soul calling is your unique way of contributing
your combination of wisdom and life force to humanity and
beyond, to all of creation. *What message have you come to share?*

You are a beacon of light in darkness. You are the hands of
love and voice of compassion. You are here to come into union
with others. You are here to bring peace.

ANGEL SUPER POWERS

Archangel Gabriel teaches you to *always* connect with Spirit.
Spirit is all-inclusive, meaning angels, God, divine love, and
you! Your essence is divine love. Micah, the Angel of Divine
Plan, provides access to your genius code. Receive the guidance and resources that are poised and ready to flow into your
divine mind, your hands of light, your loving heart. Your

angels guide each thought, action, interaction, and situation in life.

Know your Self! Angel Remiel activates your Angel Super Powers as you call them forth in daily life. They are the qualities of your Master Self:

- Peace in any situation.
- Joy regardless of how life looks.
- Unconditional love in the face of challenge.
- Unshakable faith.
- Belief in the power and presence of Spirit as the guiding force in your life.
- Compassion for the suffering of others.
- Generosity of your time, wisdom, energy, love, and stuff even when it seems like you have nothing to give. Your Self is your greatest gift.
- Fortitude, determination, and courage when the floor beneath you quakes with change!
- Relentlessness. You seek truth and love in every situation, knowing that a higher possibility is waiting to be discovered.

THE LITTLE BOOK OF ANGEL HEALING

HOW DO THESE QUALITIES TRANSLATE INTO YOUR SOUL CALLING?

Your soul calling is your credo for living, your passion, and purpose. It can be distilled into a few words that radiate your soul qualities. This message beats your heart, flows in your blood, and breathes life into every moment. While it may be invisible to you, this message shines brightly, calling forth your tribe.

We're attracted to the light we see in kindred spirits. As we come together and the light grows, we experience cocreative community. We need each other to activate our genius and empower the creative expression of soul purpose together.

WHAT IS YOUR MESSAGE?

The words in your message are encoded with light language and sacred geometry to activate a series of events that will blow your mind! You are needed! Your love and light are needed *now!* It is time for light workers to rise up in oneness to say, "Love one another!" Welcome to the *Seventh Gateway Initiation,* transferring authority to your Master Self.

ANGEL PRESCRIPTION: EMPOWER YOUR SOUL PURPOSE MESSAGE

Practice this meditation each morning to choose greater service:

- **Breathe** into your heart to feel the love that lives within you. Your loving heart is the gateway to your Soul and all the forces of creation.
- **Activate** your genius code by speaking your message. Feel Micah, the Angel of Divine Plan, by your right shoulder inspiring, guiding, and empowering you. Tune in to Archangel Gabriel by your left shoulder. Open your heart to Remiel, who brings the knowledge needed for your next steps.

- **Call forth your divine plan.** Blocks are cleared. Now is the time!
- **Call forth** your power to create through love. Call forth your healing gifts. Call forth the abundance needed to manifest your soul purpose. It's already in position, poised to pour into your heart and hands for manifestation! Money, love, support, skills, community, blessings, and guidance all here for you now. Say *yes!*
- **Activate your divine plan.** Speak your message out loud! Feel the energy stirring in the power and knowing of the words. Imagine the vibration of your message radiating outward to bless you, your family, friends, and community. Expand the benefit of your message to your city, state, country, planet, and multiverse beyond! Then bring it back into your heart and life multiplied.
- **Open** your heart and mind to receive your next steps. Journal to receive the words of guidance and energy of resource for your soul purpose. Then do it!

ANGEL BLESSING: SPEAK YOUR MESSAGE OF LOVE

We need you NOW to Shine Brightly with the radiance of divine love.

We need you to use your healing hands and speak your message of love.

We need you to be the Presence of Peace and sanity in the midst of craziness.

We need you to TRUST that there is a greater plan unfolding for humanity as institutions and beliefs are shaken.

We need you to stand on the High Road of Love as a beacon of Truth for your family, friends, and community.

We love you!

We honor you!

We respect you.

We admire your courage!

We are humble servants who love you deeply.

We are YOU and you are WE!

Want more? Visit *www.WorkingWithAngels.info.*

21.

OPEN MY HEART
TO LOVE

*I feel the love and comfort of the angels. I am so blessed.
Open my heart more! How can I walk through life in
your embrace?*

Mother Mary, the Queen of Angels, leads the Grace Angels to reveal how blessing others opens the heart and life to more love. Chamuel, the Angel of Adoration, encourages self-love and deeply loving others through Blessings and Grace. The *Fifth Gateway Initiation* has called you to anchor the source of divine love into daily life.

Rev. Jodi Cross received a message from God during The Angel Ministry training that said, "Give your heart the gift of life, fill it with unconditional love. Let it flow over and fill your entire life so that you may give your love to others and let their love shine as brightly as yours." Mother Mary guided me to make it a part of *Bring the People Back to My Love: Rosary for the Children of Light*.

GRACE ANGELS

By asking how to walk through life in the embrace of love, you are aligned with Mother Mary's invitation. Chamuel, the Angel of Adoration, said as we awaken, we are reunited in love. Love is the field of cocreation. When we sing the same tone, we vibrate at the same frequency. We become one in the harmony of love. All aspects of Self align in the song of creation.

Divine love descends from your Master Self through your soul and personality. Amarushaya, the Blessings Angel, invites you to thank all past experiences for bringing you to this moment of incarnation *as* divinity. Feel yourself transformed, new and radiantly powerful in the divinity of the Holy Self. You *are* the blessing.

You have invited the holy Self to incarnate into the physical body. The holy Self has agreed. The holy Self breathes into the soul. The Soul Star (see Chapter 3) expands to hold the brilliant presence of Divinity. Feel the warmth of this light shining on your face, illuminating the galaxy. The Soul Star pours its presence through your crown chakra, descending down the spinal cord, through the nervous system, into bones, muscles, glands, and organs. Every cell of your physical body is healed, aligned, illumined, activated with pure love.

Ananchel, the Grace angel, smiles as Heavenly Father and Holy Mother are reunited in the sacred temple of your body and life on earth. Divinity is fully incarnate in you. The holy Self has descended into matter. Your personality has been elevated into divinity. It is accomplished.

ANGEL PRESCRIPTION: ARCHANGEL CHAMUEL'S ADORATION AND WORTHINESS ACTIVATION

- **Place a hand** over your belly button. Gently move the skin in small counterclockwise circles. Chamuel is activating a facet of the sacral chakra that allows you to feel worthy. Cast out old beliefs that cause you to feel abandoned, unloved, alone, unworthy, punished, ashamed, guilty, resentful, judgmental, and fearful.
- **Get upgraded!** Chamuel is upgrading your soul contract, allowing you to expand into new states of being. Run joyfully into the arms of divine love. You are worthy.
- **Place your other hand** over your high heart, just below your clavicle. Gently move the skin in small clockwise circles, activating this chakra. A facet of the heart is opening to adoration. Can you feel how adored you are?
- **Unite with infinite love.** With one hand at your belly button, gently move the skin in one counterclockwise circle. With your other hand on your high heart, move the skin in one clockwise circle, making a figure eight. Repeat this several times, feeling the energy of the sacral chakra connect with the energy of the heart in infinite love.

- **Feel love** flowing. This is the marriage of Worthiness and Adoration. Old paradigms are released so truth can take root and flourish in you. This truth is love, joy, peace, fulfillment, enthusiasm, compassion, and other qualities of your Master Self.
- **Live each day** guided by your heart, choosing love, cherishing your connection with people, Spirit, and Love. So it is.

Want more? Visit *www.ArchangelChamuelActivation.info.*

ANGEL BLESSING: ARCHANGEL CHAMUEL PRAYER FOR SELF-LOVE AND ACCEPTANCE

Most beloved Archangel Chamuel,
teach me to love and accept myself from the inside out, to see myself as you do.
You, of the purest, highest octave of love and adoration, please infuse every layer of my being with your golden pink ray of unconditional love and acceptance.

Shine it into every cell of my body so that I might
learn how to treat this temple with respect and tenderness.
Purify my mind and emotions of patterns of neglect, self-judgment, and harsh expectations, and surrender me into the peace of a trusting, open heart.
Enfold me and the hurting disowned parts of myself in the warmth of your compassionate embrace that a healing re-union may occur.

Reveal within me the truth of my perfection right
now, as I am, and deliver me from the need to look
outside myself for validation of my worth.
Empower me with such a strong and unwavering love
that I honor my own authenticity, cherishing it as a
rare and precious jewel.

Glorious Chamuel, I give thanks for your radiant
Presence in my life and for the joyful assurance it brings
to my heart and soul.
May you be blessed a thousand-fold.
Amen.

—Rev. Bobbe Bramson, *365 Days of Angel Prayers*

22.

I Feel Livid
with Rage!

I feel victimized by how I was treated in this situation.

Often when we feel enraged, our invisible boundaries have been crossed. We feel victimized. This kind of experience is directing you to discover your soul qualities of Worthiness, Fortitude, Courage, and Determination.

Rage is a form of darkness that simply lacks love. It is a misunderstanding of unworthiness. By loving what seems to be unlovable and unworthy of love, you are lighting up the darkness. Don't love the darkness itself; don't love cruelty and bad behavior. Rather, love your Self and the true Being that is lost beneath the shallow layer of pain and fear.

Life is presenting opportunities to shine the light of love into fear and pain. Judgment is fear. Anger is pain. Guilt, shame, bitterness, resentment, cruelty, and bullying cover up deep pain of unworthiness and fear underneath the bad behavior.

PEACE ANGELS

The first responder in a crisis is Archangel Michael, protecting you. Do you feel safe in life? Do you feel secure within yourself? You are a powerful child of Light. You are entitled to love, respect, and support. Michael's Safety Activation will help you feel empowered by the flow of pure divine energy.

Do you love and value yourself? When you feel victimized, the Worthiness Angel is guiding you to unconditional love. Once you feel safe and worthy, the Peace Angel guides you to shine the light of unconditional love into the hearts of those who are suffering. Release the rage, be at peace.

This is what angels do. They see beyond the behavior and beliefs that are on the surface, to the heart that beats underneath. Through compassionate love, they release the soul from the prison of pain to be healed in the light of divine love.

You may still have judgments and other natural human feelings as your personality responds. Angel Stamera invites you to lift up your thoughts to the Almighty and divine love, calling forth the Presence to do the work of forgiveness and restoring balance. This is Angel Magic—Alchemy. You don't need to be perfect, or fully enlightened or ascended. You don't need to personally forgive the unforgivable. You don't need to agree or resign or submit to ways of thinking that are different from your own.

Angels show you how to respect and accept your differences. Invite the light of unconditional love to shine into the situation for all concerned to be the adjusting factor, working the alchemy of transformation. Each of us is unique, both in the heavens and on earth. Our unique perspectives give all of creation a wealth of variation that is spectacular!

Respect uniqueness. Accept diversity. Treasure the gift of life in all forms. This is your destiny with angels.

ANGEL PRESCRIPTION: ARCHANGEL MICHAEL'S SAFETY ACTIVATION

- **Locate** your solar plexus. With one hand, find the lowest point on your breastbone. It's the soft spot between the ribs. Archangel Michael activates this chakra to allow it to receive the flow of entitlement. You are entitled to know your divine heritage; to remember more of who you truly are; to be empowered by the flow of pure divine energy.

- **Archangel Michael is here.** Mighty and powerful in the ways of the Lord, Michael is here to set you free! You are a powerful child of the Most High! You are wise, abundant, loving, and creative. You are entitled to love, respect, and support. This is an opportunity to release memories of many lifetimes of feeling abandoned, alone, and angry.

- **Choose again!** Choose loving connections for this is your divine heritage and right. Your angels are here for you. They are supporting you, guiding you, loving you as you discover how amazing you truly are.

- **Root chakra**. Place a hand on your tailbone. Michael activates a facet of your root chakra. This center receives the energy of safety and trust. This activation will also open the base of trust in divine guidance and intervention, making it easier for you to recognize and trust in the presence and guidance of your angels.

- **Trust-Safety-Connection** form an important pyramid of Presence. You will love how this energy feels as it flows through your body. You are loved far more than you know!

ANGEL BLESSING: THE GOLDEN AGE OF ENLIGHTENMENT

All of the foundation has been laid for the dawning of the Golden Age of Enlightenment.

As a Master Soul, Master Alchemist, it is you who is manifesting the Golden Age on Earth.

Everything you touch with love turns to the gold of loving awareness—of Enlightenment, literally lighting up.

The light you carry in your soul and heart, the light you shine on others through loving care, acceptance, and respect is Enlightenment.

Each act of kindness you do is Enlightenment, lighting up a person, place, or situation that was in the darkness of ignorance.

You are a very precious beloved child of Light. We are a great family of Light as we commune in the oneness of love. You are the blessing and the gift.

23.

I Feel
So Alone!

*Hold me. I need help with an overwhelming feeling
of aloneness deep inside. I need confirmation that the
angels are with me. Am I even on the right path?*

Angel Shekinah holds you in *union* with divine love. The
Companionship Angels guide you from loneliness to Love,
understanding the longing of the soul as a beneficial force,
and recognizing the power of hope to transform. Loneliness is
a hazard of the *Fourth Gateway Initiation.* You have gone too
far into dissolution. It's time to connect with your soul family.

The call of the soul comes in many ways. Sometimes it's
a dramatic experience of revelation. It can be a deep inner
knowing. There is another type of soul's call that goes unrec-
ognized. Loneliness is its hallmark. We can lose interest in life
and feel abandoned, and not want to live. These feelings indi-
cate that *your soul is rising to the surface and trying to emerge.*
You are feeling the Longing of the Soul.

The deepest desire of the soul is to reunite with God.
You feel that desire as loneliness or a feeling that something

is missing that nothing can satisfy. Do you feel like nobody gets you? Are you different from everyone you know? Are you longing to return to a full connection of divine love?

UNITY ANGELS

Your awakening has begun. The Unity Angels are lifting you up into the embrace of divine love. The energy in loneliness is the love. That feeling of heartache is love reaching out for you. Divine love is cracking open the limitations of your heart so that you can feel your connection with Home.

I introduced the Angel of Longing in *Angel Love Cards*: "The angel of Longing can help you understand the beneficial force of this emotion that can feel so heart wrenching. Longing is your soul calling you toward love and truth. The soul's greatest desire is to return home to the heart of creation."

Longing and loneliness can either cripple you or propel you into action, motivating you to seek love. Angel Hadraniel is softening your heart to unconditional Love. The Angel of Companionship holds you in her embrace, like a mother comforting a child. Phanuel, the Angel of Hope, lights up the darkness with the promise of healing. You are a healer, and this is a time of healing!

Shekinah, the Angel of Unity, is calling you Home to your soul family. You are always in the presence of pure Love. You are never alone! You are always in the company of angels. Your soul is calling you to dispel the collective belief that you are separate from divine love and other people. You just need new friends!

ANGEL PRESCRIPTION: SPIRITUAL BUDDY

Revised from a message received by Judith Coates in *Jeshua: The Personal Christ, Vol. IV*:

- **Affirm** often: "I am not alone; I am in the presence of pure Love in this moment. I am in the presence of the love of the guides, teachers, masters, angels, the saints, and all of the loved ones I have known in any lifetime."

- **Journey** to Raphael's Healing Clinic. Your Master Self waits for you with loving connection.

- **Call a spiritual buddy.** Call a friend, first in your heart seeking a feeling of loving connection and comfort. Then call your friend on the phone and say, "I need some help. Will you help me to feel connected in love?" There is no greater purpose in life than to be with each other in love.

- In this connection of love, **describe** to your friend or angel what you want to experience. There is nothing wrong with you! Simply ask for the companionship or friendship or spiritual family that your heart and soul long for.

- **Feel deep peace.** Through the power of love, peace will surround you. The feeling of heaviness and sorrow will melt.

ANGEL BLESSING: ANGEL PRAYER
FOR FRIENDSHIP

Dear Angels,

I come to you now for my friends that I have on my
heart today.

Please bring joy to decrease their sadness.

Please bring hope when they feel lost.

Please heal their body when they are sick.

Please fill them with light when they are in the dark.

Please calm their brain when in anxiety.

Please soothe their soul when in grief
and dry their tears when
they cry.

Please help them
feel loved
when alone.

Please bring comfort
when in pain.

Please bring strength
when weak.

Please guard and guide.

And most of all,

help them to know the Grace of God

all the days of their lives.

For this I pray.

And so it is.

Amen.

—Giuliana Melo, *365 Days of Angel Prayers*

24.

HELP US TO
RESOLVE CONFLICT!

*I'm facing a painful situation with my family/work/
friends. How can we come together in truth to heal?*

Conflict happens when our invisible boundary lines have been
crossed. Boundaries are ideas about how "it" should be, concepts about how we should treat each other, and safety issues.
Perhaps you were in a situation where your expectations
weren't met. An argument may have left you feeling upset or
unloved. You may feel betrayed or threatened.

In one phase of development, we force others to believe
as we do to validate our self-worth. This need is so strong that
conflict escalating to violence, and even war, can result. As we
awaken in consciousness, we get an expanded perspective.

HARMONY ANGELS

Humility Angels remind you that you are not in control of
anyone else, nor are they in control of you. Respect Angels
guide you into spiritual maturity where you can hold space

for other perspectives, while finding strength in your own. By opening to a higher truth, you can find resolution.

We are at the forefront of a new society based on collaboration, cooperation, and creativity. What if we could seek innovation to solve underlying problems, rather than trying to defeat an opponent? Angel Charmiene guides you into harmony in your self first. Compassion Angels help you hear the other person with an open heart.

Albert Einstein said, "[A] new type of thinking is essential if mankind is to survive and move toward higher levels." Angel Amitiel assists us in finding the common thread of truth for resolution. The Angels of Illumination guide us into a quantum leap into cocreative society as we work together for the highest good of all.

ANGEL PRESCRIPTION: THE ILLUMINED SELF

Revised from a powerful message received through Judith Coates in *Jeshua: The Personal Christ, Vol. IV:*

- **Breathe.** Relax. The Angels of Illumination are helping you to witness the situation from the heavenly realm. Allow your eyes and mouth to relax; allow them to become soft. Take another breath, inhaling deeply and gently. Breathe out slowly. Feel a state of calm as you relax. Breathe in and out. Begin to feel at peace.
- **Become a witness.** Allow your breathing to be expansive and gentle. Feel the light all around you, a soft and loving golden white light that illuminates everything. Breathe into this light, allowing your mind to expand. In this sacred place of peace, become a witness. Review

what happened in your mind's eye and watch it replay. What did they say or do to you? How did that feel? What did you say or do to them? How did you feel about your part?

- **Illuminate the scene.** This time, see yourself and the other person as light bodies. Imagine each of you as a vortex of light energy, flashing and pulsating. Is it white or colorful? See the energy exchange in the encounter. What was their energy like as they spoke to you? What was your energy like as you listened? What was your energy like as you responded either verbally or silently? Does it have colors? In what shape is the energy flowing? How are your energies interacting?

- **Speak from your heart.** In this expanded state of witnessing the interplay of energy, what do you feel in your heart? What would your heart say to that person? As you allow your heart to speak, witness how the energy responds. How does it feel? Do the colors or patterns of light change? What action would your heart take? Watch the energy and feel the transformation.

- **Accept the blessing.** As the energy transforms, allow the blessings of healing and respect to be present in this sacred place of peace. Taking another deep breath, invite the angels to illuminate both of you with harmony, compassion, truth, respect, and humility. Breathe. Relax. Bring yourself back to the present moment feeling peaceful, feeling healed.

- **Watch for opportunities for resolution.** The next time you see the other person, be open for resolution.

ANGEL BLESSING: IGNITE YOUR LEADERSHIP

Enter into Abundance mindset, connection and flow.
Am I in a state of love and abundance?
Am I grounded in the safety and security of divine
    energy?

Ignite Leadership based in love.
I am a powerful creator of my experience.
My ideas are literally the seeds of creation.

I am the Hero of my own story.
I channel the divine energy of my
    true self into the world.
There is tangible substance and truth
    in my vision before I see results.

My community is mobilized.
My heart and love let me connect
    with people in true and
    vulnerable ways.
In joyful thanksgiving, we focus on
    solutions while the flow is still invisible.

I amp up my success frequency!
What if everything I do is about receiving the gift of
Love from God?
Success is the culmination of heart and spirit coming
    together for the benefit of all.

—paraphrased from Karen Tax, *The IAM Way,*
the IAM Way Compass

25.

HUNGER

*It hurts my heart to see people going hungry. What can
I do to help those who are suffering from hunger?*

Hunger is all around us. It's the guy on the corner with a sign
saying, "Anything will help." It's on the face of one in six children at the school down the street from your house. It's the
parent who has to decide to pay the utility bill or buy groceries
to feed the kids. While hunger is interconnected with poverty,
weather-related events like fire, floods, and hurricanes affect
food availability and distribution. When we watch the news,
where there is conflict, there are food shortages.

Supply Angels call forth mercy for those who are suffering
and feel vulnerable, generosity from the world in response,
and prosperity of every good thing to relieve the situation and
bring needed healing.

Experts agree that *there is more than enough food to feed
everyone.* Add to that eleven billion pounds of garden produce
that becomes waste annually. So why aren't we outraged that
815 million people are malnourished?

What does this mean to you? Are you feeling called to help feed hungry neighbors and kids? This is not hopeless; there are ways that you can help.

SUPPLY ANGELS

Ooniemme invites you to feel grateful for the food supply and food security that you have. Make a *gratitude list* of everything that contributes to your being well fed, including money flow from jobs, friends, and family. Add appreciation for all areas of abundance with Fortunata, the Angel of Prosperity.

Now, what to do about hunger? The Angel of Vulnerability helps you identify the vulnerable population that you wish to serve. My community noticed that there were a surprising number of homeless and hungry teens. The Answer For Youth, or TAFY, was created, providing a place for them to hang out with food and necessities. Local churches and people bring hot meals and provide for other needs regularly.

When you see weather events, economic downturns, and conflict on TV, you are seeing a short-term food crisis in the making. Generosity Angels invite you to participate generously in some way. Food banks and feeding programs always need volunteers and contributions.

Are you an innovator? Can you inspire your community to turn a vacant lot into a small farm with free produce for everyone? Many programs are springing up that encourage planting "food not lawns" in public places as well as front yards. In a better world, we could walk down the street and pick the food we need to be fed today.

AmpleHarvest.org was created to end food waste and hunger in America: "Our online search function enables backyard gardeners to share their fresh healthy food with local food pantries." Are you the go-between? Does your grocery store toss food that is about to expire in a dumpster? Or does it send the food to a feeding project? What local churches and organizations offer feeding programs? What do local commercial farmers do after harvest? Do they allow gleaning? Who gleans and where does the food go?

ANGEL PRESCRIPTION: BE A FOOD ACTIVIST

Go from wishful thinking to active participant! You are needed.

- **Identify** the vulnerable population you feel called to feed, whether local or distant.
- **Take action.** What can you do? Can you donate food, money, or time? Can you cook or serve? Can you connect individuals with groups that support a common cause?
- **Respond generously.** If it doesn't seem like you have the time, energy, or resources to actively participate, prayer is a powerful response.
- **Do something!** What about popping a few cans of beans into the collection box at the grocery store around holidays? Fire stations and churches have food drives. Watch for the collection boxes and add something from your own grocery bag. You can do it.

ANGEL BLESSING: A PRAYER FOR WORLD PEACE

Beloved Angels,
Guide our hearts in remembrance of who we really are,
beings of love and light—made from the same source.

Let our spiritual DNA spring forth with acceptance for
all paths as all paths are one path: and remind us that
what we hold as the only way, interweaves with the
mystical path of truth.

Flood our world with love and light so that each soul
awakens in remembrance of one human family: one
    spiritual ancestry.
Send us the grace of the open heart so we may heal from
    loss and find again the way to love.

Shower us with blessings.
Enfold us in wings of starlight; be beside us as we walk
upon the earth, and remind us to tread lightly with
honor and gratitude for all that we have been given.

Awaken us to the dawn of a completely new day, one
filled with all the potential the universe holds. Guide
us to live this day as if it were the first day, the only
day—for that is what it is.
Give us today the gift of peace.
And so it is.

—Cathleen O'Connor, PhD, *365 Days of Angel Prayers*

26.

VIOLENCE

I'm watching with horror as another atrocity unfolds. What can I do to lessen the suffering from these acts of violence?

Whether you are in the middle of domestic or other violence, feeling the pain of a family member, or witnessing violence play out somewhere in the world, *you are authorized and empowered to invoke Divine Intervention!* First responder Archangel Michael brings Protection! Archangel Uriel is on the scene providing personal assistance for both victims and perpetrators. The Justice Angel team adds the strength of Purity to honor all feelings and experiences. Mihr helps to restore Relationships and Harmony.

Violent people are in pain. They are deeply wounded and see nothing but despair. Anger turns to blame and vengefulness becomes aggression. People caught in the energy vibration of rage can't escape it. From rage, there are no other possibilities but sharing pain by hurting others.

Are you in an abusive relationship? Abuse can be physical, emotional, mental, or financial. Verbal threats and demeaning accusations are abusive. Is your spouse jealous and controlling? Do you need to get permission to talk to friends or go anywhere? Does your spouse dictate what you wear and how you behave? Does your abuser control the money so you don't have any? Seek professional help and get out. Resources and support are available.

JUSTICE ANGELS

You are a healer. Each time you experience or witness violence, you are on the first responder team with Archangel Uriel. Be the willing servant who responds to the needs of others the best you can in the moment. Often the response is through prayer.

Breathe into your holiness and connect with the Source of Unconditional Love. Know that everyone involved is also holy. Archangel Michael is already on the scene with protection. He is there bringing comfort to those who are leaving the body and those who survive. Mihr, the Angel of Relationship, comforts family, friends, responders, and community. We often see communities come together in action and compassion to support the recovery and healing of those who are directly impacted by mass violence. Angel Charmiene brings the community into resonant harmony as new ways to provide mental health services and forgiveness bring healing.

Trauma from violent experiences can cause brain-based dysfunctions, and brain-based therapies can bring about the most effective healing. Lori Leyden, PhD, MBA, is recognized as a global leader in responding to trauma from violence with survivors of the Rwanda genocide, the Sandy Hook Elementary School shooting, the Marjory Stoneman Douglas High School shooting, and more. With her Rapid Response Trauma Healing team, she has seen that post-traumatic stress disorder (PTSD) is just as damaging to those who treat the survivors.

Dr. Leyden has pioneered evidence-based trauma healing protocols with EFT/Tapping, a brain-based therapy. If you are experiencing trauma from violence either first or second hand, seek professional assistance. Don't suffer alone.

ANGEL PRESCRIPTION: YOU ARE AN EMPOWERED HEALER

- **Breathe.** Let your body relax. You are safe. Let your thoughts relax. Breathe into your heart and let it relax. Feel your soul and the angels surrounding you, protecting you.
- **Elevate your consciousness.** Breathe into your soul, your Soul Star, and your Master Self to become the witness. See the events unfolding as a dance of energy. Keep going to the heavenly realm where legions of angels await your command.

- **It's you!** You are authorized and empowered to invoke Divine Intervention and healing for everyone, including perpetrators. See everyone as holy, just as you are. See this situation as an opportunity to heal and elevate consciousness for all.
- **Command** divine protection, safety, comfort, and healing. Trust your healer's heart to know what is needed. The angels are responding.
- **See it done.** In your imagination, see it done. Open your eyes. Move on.

ANGEL BLESSING: ONE WITH OUR WORLD

Describing the *Sixth Gateway Initiation*, Dr. Leyden said, "We must fall in love with ourselves and our world as we are now. From this open-hearted place of nonresistance to what is, we can begin the work of healing ourselves and our world."

My God is your God
My religion is gratitude, love, joy and wonder

When I am:
One with my Breath
One with my Body
One with my Heart
One with my World

We can be:
One with our Breath
One with our Bodies
One with our Hearts
One with our World

—Lori Leyden, PhD, MBA, *The Grace Process™ Guidebook*

27.

POLITICAL
UNREST

I can't sleep and feel nauseated from what I see in our political system. At the same time, I'm feeling empowered to step up as a new leader of Light!

Focus on envisioning a society you want to live in. Visualize our local, national, and global leaders as diverse, kind, and wise. Imagine a thriving business world that serves humanity with abundance for all and innovation that solves challenges.

What can you do to make this world your reality? You are being called to serve humanity on the *Sixth Gateway Initiation.* How can you change your own life to fulfill your vision? What small steps can you take that will benefit others?

ACTION ANGELS

You are witnessing chaos created by those who are disconnected from the Source of Wisdom and Love. While it is unpleasant and can even appear frightening at times, Angel Kaeylarae says, "Be at *peace.*" Be the Peacemaker.

This chaos is part of the cycle of elevating consciousness. Not everyone is ready to forsake ego control and shift to Divine Presence. As you witness this unfolding, have compassion for the public figures that are struggling to retain power and control. Witness the mischief they create with a philosophy of greed. In the bigger picture, they are disrupting the status quo—opening space for the new energy to pour in so that beneficial change can occur. Angel Hadraniel invites you to put on *love* glasses. Infuse the collective consciousness with kindness and hope. Be the Lover.

When you identify a player whose actions destroy systems, hurting people, Angel Paschar is activating your divine vision. Wonder, how can this situation be resolved? What innovative strategies elevate us all to the level of care and collaboration we need? Be the Visionary.

Kind-hearted people are awakening to the need to care for their fellow humans. The true role of government is to care for the needs of the people! Action Angels are inspiring millions of us to find our voices within the system. Millions of citizens are realizing our power to choose. We have the means to care for one another, for we are all truly One. That is where the expression "one another" came from. Every one of us, even those we disagree with and disdain, have a purpose. By stirring up the systems, they are opening the way for true reform that is respectful of all.

We are at the dawning of a new Golden Age. Angels are here en masse to elevate our consciousness, inspire right action, and uplift us into divine experience. The Action Angels are revealing steps you can take to improve relationships in your local area, state, country, and planet. Be the Activist.

ANGEL PRESCRIPTION:
BE A SPIRITUAL ACTIVIST

- **Be a visionary.** Visualize what you want to see in the political system that most interests you. It may be global, national, statewide, or local. By taking an interest and imagining what you would like to see, you are contributing to the collective consciousness of possibility.

- **Be an opportunist.** Focus on opportunities for positive change. Keep your attention on the possibilities for a better life for all.

- **Be an activist.** Join groups that align with your vision. Take action as you feel called. Contribute, attend, march, volunteer, vote, speak, participate.

- **Be a force of love.** Love is the most powerful force in all of creation. By radiating your loving heart, you are feeding the collective consciousness for all humanity with kindness, compassion, generosity, and hope.

- **Be on the leading edge.** What can you do in your life to create a better, more sustainable future? Grow a food garden, get an electric car, install a rainwater capture system on your home, put up solar panels, volunteer, reduce unnecessary consumption.

- **Be joyful!** Play! Have more fun. Increase your personal community of friends. Join groups that do or support things you enjoy. Open your heart to connect more deeply and personally with people.

- **Be a peacemaker.** Make friends with someone who has a different lifestyle and beliefs than you do. Humanizing people who are different reduces fear and fosters peace.

ANGEL BLESSING: BE LOVE IN
THE WORLD TODAY

You are Loved.
You are The Lover!
You ARE the LOVE!
Breathe into your heart.
Can you feel the love in the air?
Can you feel love caressing your skin?
Breathe.
Can you feel love circulating in the oxygen in your body?
Can you sense the space between the molecules of your
   body vibrating in love?
This is the Truth, there is only Love.
We are with you every moment of eternity, embracing
   you with love.

You are Love!

How can you BE LOVE in the world today?
Silently radiating the love that is a powerful presence in
   your heart?
Actively through your speech and actions with others?
Be mindful of your words, thoughts,
   and actions.
Make them a living prayer—
   an expression of love.
What would love say?
What would love do?

BE LOVE.

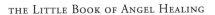

28.

ANIMALS

My best friend is struggling. I can't stand to watch animals suffer!

Hold a purring kitty in your lap to feel comforted. Your dog looks at you with those deep brown eyes, or maybe a blue one, and you feel seen. Some say that early humans wouldn't have survived without companion animals. If your primary relationship in life is with an animal, you know this to be true.

Whether furred, winged, hooved, or scaled, domestic or wild, animals communicate telepathically through feelings, images, and essence. Their biggest gift is teaching you to be present with them. Return the honor. Give your friend your full attention when you tend, feed, groom, play, and hang out together. They don't multitask with you, unless something more interesting scampers by: "Squirrel!"

COMPANION ANGELS

Angels hold every form of life in a tender embrace. Call on Ariel, the Angel of Nature, to help you communicate with your animals. Animals know angels. Our companion animals love us unconditionally. Animals care for us and often take on our illnesses as a gift of loving compassion.

Is your best friend suffering health or behavior issues? This is an invitation to heal together. Did you know that animals have Guardian Angels, too? Ask your Guardian Angel to connect with theirs to help with understanding and healing.

What does your friend need? You may sense images or emotions. Body position provides clues. You can't miss it when they are hungry or want to go out. What else are they telling you through attitude and behavior? When we don't get the message, animals escalate with behavior issues and illness, often reflecting the stress they feel from you.

Breathe. Relax. Hang out together with no agenda. Allow yourself to "just know" what your friend is telling you. Archangel Raphael delights in holding our beloved friends in the green light of healing love.

When you see fires, floods, and other disasters in the news, animals have been left behind and need rescue. Archangel Michael sends blue protective energy into situations of danger, abuse, neglect, and natural disasters. You are in the *Sixth Gateway Initiation* when you care deeply about animals and watch for opportunities to direct healing love to them. We learn deeper trust and can open our hearts to animals in ways that we can't with humans.

ANGEL PRESCRIPTION: RAPHAEL'S GREEN LIGHT HEALING

Hold small animals in your lap, sit or stand next to larger animals, or direct this healing energy to animals at a distance. They get it! (Inspired by Linda Kean, animal communicator)

- **Pet your friend.** Speak softly with a comforting tone explaining that you and the angels are going to help with the pain, distress, or issue. Relax and breathe.
- **Imagine** lighting up the chakras connecting you and your friend energetically.
- **Raphael's orb of green light** floats toward you. Archangel Raphael is opening a portal to heal you both. Golden pink loving warmth comes through as Ariel joins you.
- **The angels carry** both your souls up through the heavenly realms to the highest source energy. You can feel your Master Selves connecting in golden pink love.
- **Protection** from Archangel Michael enters the healing space and the animal if it is at risk.
- **Let go.** Raphael's green light grows to surround you both. The green pulls energy through your chakras. It is easy to let go of everything that isn't for the highest and best of both of you.

- **Anchor the love bond.** Ariel directs pink love light through every cell of your friend, growing stronger as disease is removed. Ariel infuses healing light between you. Feel the bond of love strengthening.
- **Release worries** for your pet and his or her worries for you. Archangel Michael adds the golden light of hope, understanding, and joy to the healing energy. Fill your mind with happy, healthy images of the two of you playing. Love and healing fuse together, creating deep healing for your souls. Animals know this light and can heal instantly.
- **Relax in love.** The angels seal in the healing love and guide you back through the realms to your bodies. Ariel touches your third eye to ground you. Raphael touches the top of your heads to send the healing from your soul chakras down to your root. It is done.

ANGEL BLESSING:
A PRAYER FOR ANIMALS

We call on Archangel Raphael to assist any animals with special needs and we observe their perfection now.

We ask Archangel Michael to safely guide any lost or missing pets back into the loving arms of their families and friends.

With Archangel Chamuel's peaceful presence, we see the animals passing on to the next leg of their journey, doing so blissfully and gently.

We give thanks that Mother Mary looks after our animal welfare organizations and all of the souls working to provide nurturing, life-long homes for surrendered pets.

We enjoy seeing our wildlife thrive, living in healthy, balanced ecosystems with the abundant blessings of Archangel Ariel and the nature spirits.

We are forever grateful to God for gifting us with these sacred beings of pure, unconditional love.

We give thanks to St. Francis that our hearts, minds, and ears are open to their intuitive whispers and that we may continue to honor them in the highest and best ways.

We are open and receptive.
We welcome any miracles with a grateful heart.

—Marla Steele, *365 Days of Angel Prayers*

29.

NATURAL
DISASTERS

I'm witnessing a devastating force of weather, earthquake, or fire. What can I do to help mitigate the situation?

We humans are delicate and precariously balanced. It doesn't take much to decimate our homes and lives. What if natural occurrences were a blessing and a do-over instead of a catastrophe? Werner Erhard called this a "benestrophe." *If you are affected by a situation, your soul is inviting you to contribute.* You may be living the experience personally or watching a situation unfold somewhere in the world. Bring your light to transform it. Feel yourself One with the possibility of benevolent-catastrophe.

Expand your sense of self to encompass the area affected, the continent, the planet, the solar system, the Milky Way galaxy, the universe, the heavens! You are divine love. You are radiantly powerful in the divinity of your holy Self. Breathe radiant love and peace from the heavenly realm, into our universe, Milky Way galaxy, solar system, our pale blue dot planet Earth, the affected continent and area, and into your home and life.

NATURE ANGELS

Call upon Archangel Michael to protect the people in harm's way. Link your Guardian Angel with those affected. They will be strengthened and encouraged by your loving compassion and vision. When an area has been reduced to rubble, we have the opportunity to raise our sights together. How can benevolence result from catastrophic loss? Imagine families strengthened in love. Envision businesses generously contributing resources and innovation. Paschar guides you to visualize communities overcoming differences, finding common ground to unite in care for one another. Imagine affected communities coming together in cooperation, designing new ways to organize and build. The Angel of Courage opens your heart to benedictions in the midst of loss. Be courageous!

Ariel, the Angel of Nature, delights when we take responsibility, realizing we make a difference. *Ask!* Ask Ariel to balance the forces of nature. Move excessive rain from a flooded area to dry, burning territory. Calm the wind and waters. Relieve stress with gentle movements. Be a Force of Nature!

Generosity Angels guide us to respond to the needs of others. Send money, pray, or volunteer. Follow your heart to the response that best shares your gifts and abilities with those in need. Elon Musk modified a rocket tube to help rescue boys trapped in a cave in Thailand. Rev. Velma Alford volunteered with Red Cross, handing out toothbrushes and kindness during Hurricane Katrina near her home in Louisiana. People from all over feel called to jump in their cars with blankets, food, water, clothing, and medicine, driving to a scene where people are in need. Prayer masters devote time and energy watching news unfold, sending love, angels, healing, and comfort to disaster victims.

ANGEL PRESCRIPTION: HARNESSING BENESTROPHES

What will you do?

- **Activate your divinity** by expanding into your Master Self; then direct healing love to Mother Gaia. See her coming into balance peacefully. Appreciate her generosity.
- **Imagine opportunities** to rebuild with greater love and community.
- **Feel the connection** of oneness with those involved, holding them in comfort and encouragement.
- **Ask** Ariel and the Nature Angels to modulate the weather, better distributing wind, water, earth, and fire to support all life.
- **Volunteer.** Be courageous! Find the way that best suits you to give. Prayer at home is a powerful form of giving.
- **Be proactive.** Join the Community Emergency Response Team (CERT) in your area. Contact the Red Cross. Find out how you can prepare and respond to benestrophes in your community.

ANGEL BLESSING: BLESSED MIRACLES

Believe in your ability to create blessed miracles, each day, through Angel's Divine Love.

Still your heart as it is a sacred and holy place, where miracles can happen with clarity and deep awakening.

As you experience others' resistance and deep-rooted fears, let your heart light shine so that it brightens to heal, love, guide, and be in service for evolution.

Go forth and trust.
Our daily infusions of
    Divine Love guide you.
Love is always the answer.
Forgiveness is as necessary
    as breathing.

Surrender is as necessary as eating.
Trust is as necessary as sleeping.

Go forth with confidence as you see with clarity and experience the miracles of trusting, believing and surrendering to Divine Love by listening daily to your
    heart's voice.
You are a powerful miracle worker.
Each action you take and each thought you vibrate with Divine Love magnifies and expands into blessed miracles.

You are ready, Beloved!
Your soul wings are golden and your heart is full of
    our love.
Keep your eyes on the sky, hands on your heart,
    and feet grounded on precious Mother Earth.
Feel the vibrations of love infusing your heart for the
    birthing of new miracles.

—Rev. Lisa A. Clayton, *365 Days of Angel Prayers*

THE LITTLE BOOK OF ANGEL HEALING

30.

HELP ME TO MANIFEST THE POWERFUL VISIONS I SEE

I know my next step on my Soul Path. I see the vision and am ready to take action.

I dreamed that I met Paul McCartney. With tears in my eyes, I thanked him for providing the soundtrack for my life. He genuinely received my gratitude, creating a deep and soul-felt connection between us. As I turned to leave, he asked, "Aren't you coming with me around the world? The jet is waiting." What an invitation! I had all these excuses for why I couldn't go. I woke up perplexed.

What if you had millions of dollars, a private jet, staff, publishers, everything needed to manifest your visions? When you receive huge visions from the divine, do you have an endless list of excuses for why you can't do it? The Beatles sang about the way to get back home in their song "Golden Slumbers."

MANIFESTATION ANGELS

Our powerful vision from Paschar takes us Home. We are bringing heaven to earth with each experience of our Master Self. The resonance of divine love brings smiles to the eyes of those around us. In our golden slumbers, Archangel Jophiel provides creative power to manifest our visions here on earth. What if the resources are being provided and we just haven't learned to recognize them yet? We've been carrying that weight a long time, thinking we have to manifest our visions alone. And in the end, it's love that matters most.

Angel Jamaerah calls forth the support team, community, clients, and resources needed for manifestation. We weren't meant to do it alone. The act of cocreation is love. This is the *Seventh Gateway Initiation,* birthing our Master Self through manifesting our visions with others in participatory divinity.

We need cocreative, sacred community to manifest divine visions. According to Barbara Marx Hubbard, when we join together with kindred souls, "the drive to express our creativity will give us the energy to overcome our own limitations." Hubbard goes on to say in her book *Emergence*, "by being together we establish a 'resonant field,' which feels as though we are being connected at a deeper level with a cosmic pattern. It is a field of agape, or love."

Archangel Metatron provides Thought, Light Language, and Sacred Geometry to create the energetic frame and building blocks of that cosmic pattern. Metatron said, "Create from your heart through love and rewards will be great." Notice your dreams and take action on the clues that present in daily life. The universe is conspiring to support your sacred work!

ANGEL PRESCRIPTION:
LOVE ALWAYS FINDS A WAY

- **Willingness** unlocks the treasure vault of resources and wisdom. Know you are One with your vision. Relax your focus to move into the consciousness of your Master Self, allowing you to think outside the box.
- **Expand** your perspective beyond your limiting beliefs. Are you looking for what's right or what's wrong? Don't you want to feel the flow of seeing possibilities that you never would have thought of?
- **Access.** Your loving heart is the access point.
- **Open your heart in love**, so everything you need for your next step of your mission flows in.
- **Affirm**, "I allow abundance of time, wealth, and love to flow into my life."
- **Open** your heart often throughout the day.
- **Receive.** Check with your angel team to receive guidance and encouragement. As they say, "We are here *always!*"

ANGEL BLESSING: WELCOME TO THE COUNSEL OF THE BELOVED

Beloved child of the Most High, welcome to the Counsel of the Beloved. Take your seat with us in loving devotion and service to the One Source of all Love. We are with you always, guiding, supporting, and loving you.

When you turn away, we are here. We remain. We continue to guide, support, and love you until you complete the work that was intended.

You never really turn away; you follow a different path of study that fills an important part in the whole of your awakening. All is in divine timing and leading to the fulfillment of your divine plan.

We treasure you, Beloved One. We honor your steadfast devotion and endeavor. We are pleased that you have come to this moment, this place in consciousness, prepared for the next map on your journey.

Let the wind blow away all doubt and fear.
Let the rising sun illuminate your consciousness.
Open your heart to divine love and will.

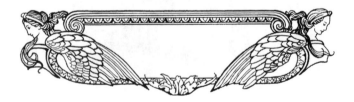

THE LITTLE BOOK OF ANGEL HEALING

Be an Earth Angel in Action

Now that you have practiced working with your angels on a daily basis to solve challenges and respond to opportunities in life, how will you continue to include angels in your daily life? And more important, how do the angels invite you to expand your service and connection?

The angels say:

We are calling our Beloved Children of Light to find each other. Come together in strength. There are millions of you. No two of you are alike. You live all around the world in every country. You practice every religion and faith. You are focused on many different ways to help each other, your planet Earth, and the heavens.

We are calling you Home, Beloved Child. Can you feel your soul yearning for Home? Can you feel your heart calling you to love? These symptoms reveal that you are a Child of Light and you are hearing our call.

We are calling the many different groups and leaders to connect in oneness. Find the common thread that binds you. Find the soul calling that unites you. We need you to gather together in larger groups. We need you to pray together. We need you to meditate together. We need you to discuss important topics that bring you together. In the strength of larger numbers, a greater power and presence of divine love can manifest.

When you gather together, you see yourselves reflected in each other's eyes. You will discover that while you may use different words, your souls are yearning for the same connection of love and oneness. Together, you will experience more of who you are. You will discover more about the gifts and abilities you have been given. You will see more of your divine plan unfolding. You will have the courage to act as you are being guided.

You stand at a very precious turning point. Will you take the leap of faith? Will you say yes to your divine calling?

You are an important piece of the whole. You are needed.

Come Home Now.
Come Home to love, oneness, guidance, healing, everything needed to fulfill your soul calling.
You are worthy and valuable.
You are loved.
Come Home to Love.

Your family of light is here. You are invited to join our *GatewayCommunityOfHigherConsciousness.com.* Empower your spiritual calling and path each month as we connect in love and joy, creativity and healing.

Resources

365 Days of Angel Prayers
- *www.youtube.com*
- *www.facebook.com*

Albert Einstein, "Atomic Education Urged by Einstein," *New York Times,* May 25, 1946.

AmpleHarvest.org, connects backyard farmers with food banks

Ani Pathik, *www.facebook.com/anita.pathik.law*

Barbara Marx Hubbard, *Emergence: The Shift from Ego to Essence,* 10 steps to the universal human

Rev. Bobbe Bramson, *www.angelhearttoheart.com*

Cathleen O'Connor, PhD, *www.cathleenoconnor.com*

Rev. Cathi Burke, *www.angeloflightministry.com*
- *Americo Michael: Surrounded By Angels—A Journey in Transformation*
- *My Soul's Embrace: A Path of Self Discovery and Healing*

David R. Hawkins, *Power vs. Force*

Debbie Ford, *The Right Questions: Ten Essential Questions to Guide You to an Extraordinary Life*

Giuliana Melo, *www.giulianamelo.com/*

Rev. Jana Marie Toutolmin, *www.facebook.com*

Jean Slatter, *Hiring the Heavens: A Practical Guide to Developing Working Relationships with the Spirits of Creation, www.Jean Slatter.com*

Rev. Jodi Cross, contributor, *Bring the People Back to My Love: Rosary for the Children of Light, rev.jodicross@gmail.com*

Judith Coates, *www.OakbridgeUniversity.org*

- *Jeshua: The Personal Christ, Volume IV: The Interdimensional Self, The Way to Peace*
- *Jeshua: The Personal Christ, Volume VII: Absolute Love, Infinite Light*

Judith Larkin Reno, PhD, *Spiritual Initiation* online course, *www. GatewayUniversity.info*

Julie Geigle, *www.heavensenthealing.us*

Karen Tax, *The IAM Way Compass, www.theiamway.com*

Kay Sheppard, "Breaking Free from Food Addiction," *www.Kay Sheppard.com*

Rev. Kimberly Marooney, PhD, *www.KimberlyMarooney.com*

- *A-HA! A unique self-help guide to Archangel-Healing Activation Sessions*
- *Angel Blessings: Cards of Sacred Guidance and Inspiration*
- *Angel Love Cards of Divine Devotion, Faith and Grace*
- *Bring the People Back to My Love: A Rosary for the Children of Light*
- *My Angel Connection: The Guidebook to Interactions with Angels*
- *Sacred Book of Light: Holy Sacraments*
- *Your Guardian Angel in a Box: Heavenly Protection, Love and Guidance*

Linda Kean, *Archangel Raphael and Ariel Healing Meditation for Animals, www.youtube.com/watch?v=yRPWkMJFFhU&t=3s*

Rev. Lisa A. Clayton, *www.LisaAClayton.com*

Lori Leyden, PhD, MBA, *www.createglobalhealing.org*

- *The Grace Process™ Guidebook*
- *Trauma Healing and Resiliency Response Team*

Louise Hay, *You Can Heal Your Life*

Rick Hanson, PhD, *www.RickHanson.net*

Samuel Barber, *Adagio for Strings*

Rev. Saxon Knight, *Seraphim Angels: Guide to the Healing Path of Love: Heal Your Life with the Power of Belief, The Teachings of the Seraphim Angels, Book Two, www.SaxonKnight.com*

Sound Essence, *Archangel Blessing Mists, www.SoundEssence.net*

Sunny Dawn Johnston, Kimberly Marooney, Karen Paolino Correia, and Roland Comtois, including Angel Messengers from Across the Globe, *365 Days of Angel Prayers, www.Sunny DawnJohnston.com*

Susan Shumsky, DD, *Instant Healing: Gain Inner Strength, Empower Yourself, and Create Your Destiny, www.DivineRevelation.org*

The Answer for Youth (TAFY), *www.theanswer4youth.org*

Timothy Conway, *Women of Power and Grace: Nine Astonishing, Inspiring Luminaries of Our Time*

Rev. Velma Alford, *www.VelmaAlford.com*

Vianna Stibal, *ThetaHealing™: Introducing an Extraordinary Energy-Healing Modality*

Vicki Synder-Young, *www.VickiSnyder.com*

ACKNOWLEDGMENTS

Nancy Owen Barton is an earth angel! She saw my vision, held my hand, and guided me through the two years it took to solidify the concept of *The Little Book of Angel Healing*, write the proposal, and share the magic until Greg Brandenburgh and Hampton Roads said YES!

Yes! The most important word in creation.

Dana, my beloved, always sees the best in me.

Lori, Karen, Jackie, and Lorraine encourage me to expand into ever-greater states of sharing divine love and wisdom.

My friends in the Gateway and Oakbridge Communities delight with me as we journey deeper into Spirit. I feel so loved, so blessed.

Most of all, you, the reader. You give me the ability to share the divine love and wisdom that lives in my heart, soul, and Master Self.

You can find me in the Healing Clinic. I'm one of those light beings, and so are YOU!